The Coors Connection

How Coors Family Philanthropy
Undermines Democratic Pluralism

RUSS BELLANT

South End Press
Boston, MA

A Political Research Associates Book

Political Research Associates
678 Massachusetts Avenue, Suite 205, Cambridge, MA 02139
(617) 661-9313

Political Research Associates is an independent research institute which collects and disseminates information on right-wing political groups and trends. Centralized in its archives is a continuously-updated collection of over one hundred right-wing publications, including newspapers, magazines, newsletters, and direct mail appeals. The institute's library contains hundreds of volumes relating to the political right wing. Also maintained are extensive files of primary and secondary material on individuals, groups, and topics of interest to those researching the right wing.

Political Research Associates offers classes on the American right wing, provides speakers for groups and conferences, publishes educational posters, and prepares, on request, specific research reports on topics pertaining to the political right wing.

The Political Research Associates Topical Report Series, co-published with South End Press, provides background information on subjects of current interest to those interested in understanding the right wing in the United States.

Political Research Associates Staff:
Jean V. Hardisty, DIRECTOR
Chip Berlet, ANALYST
Margaret Quigley, RESEARCHER/ARCHIVIST

10 9 8 7 6 5 4 3 2 1

Design, production & type by dg graphics
Cover design by David Gerratt
Cover photograph by Deborah Bright
Manufactured in the USA

Support for this report was provided by
The Funding Exchange/National Community Funds, and many individual donors.

LIBRARY OF CONGRESS CATALOGING-IN-PUBLICATION DATA
Bellant, Russ, 1949–
    The Coors connection: how Coors family philanthropy undermines democratic pluralism/ by Russ Bellant. — 2nd ed.
        p. cm.
    "A Political Research Associates Book."
    Includes bibliographical references and index.
    ISBN 0–89608–417–5 (cloth): $25.00. — ISBN 0–89608–416–7 (paper): $9.00
    1. Conservatism—United States—History—20th century.   2. Coors family—Political activity.   3. United States—Politics and government—1945—   I. Political Research Associates.   II. Title.
E839.5.B43   1991
320.5'2'0973—dc20   91–3524
                                                                         CIP

South End Press, 116 St. Botolph St., Boston, MA 02115

" *The New Right feeds on discontent, anger, insecurity, and resentment, and flourishes on backlash politics. Through its interlocking network, it seeks to veto whatever it perceives to threaten its way of life—busing, women's liberation, gay rights, pornography, loss of the Panama Canal —and promotes a beefed-up defense budget, lower taxes, and reduced federal regulation of small business. . . .*

" *The New Right network supports whoever shares its desire for radical political change and its resentments of the status quo. As such, the New Right is anything but conservative . . . .*

" *The replacement [in 1979 of the] chairman of the American Conservative Union was a reflection of an attempt by traditional conservatives within the Washington, D.C., area to minimize the influence of New Right leaders like Colorado brewer Joseph Coors, his Washington political operative Paul Weyrich, and fundraiser Richard Viguerie. . . . The attempt by New Right leaders to control the organization can be traced to Coors' decision in 1971 to bankroll right-wing organizations.* "

Alan Crawford
Thunder on the Right
1980

PREFACE

BY CHIP BERLET

C oors family philanthropy aims a financial silver bullet at the heart of democratic pluralism in the United States. The Coors family members have financed an interlocking network of ultra-conservative and far-right institutions which have gained respectability during the past decade. Few average citizens have read even a tiny portion of the mountain of literature produced by these rightist groups. Some who have acquainted themselves with these writings and their conclusions, however, have been horrified at the narrow and spiteful view of America and Americans enunciated by these zealous ideologues.

Those who have benefited, directly and indirectly, from Coors family generosity include persons whose views reflect not only traditional conservatism, but also nativism, xenophobia, theories of racial superiority, sexism, homophobia, authoritarianism, militarism, reaction, and in some cases outright neo-fascism.

These charges may seem shocking, but consider that Holly and Jeffrey Coors serve on the national board of the rightist Council for National Policy along with a former Ku Klux Klan leader and others who championed segregationist policies. In one notable case, a Coors-funded New Right leader, Paul Weyrich, sponsors the work of a convicted Nazi collaborator, Laszlo Pasztor, a Hungarian-American who built a political network of persons and groups with fascist, racist, and anti-Semitic backgrounds.

The Coors family comes to its political activism after having established a well-deserved reputation for aggressive (some would say cutthroat) business acumen, most visibly through the Coors brewery and its widely advertised beers. That the Coors name apparently opens doors in Washington, D.C. was noted in the August 7, 1989 issue of *Newsweek* in an article on the

Department of Housing and Urban Development (HUD) scandal. Along with a picture of Joe Coors, *Newsweek* ran the caption: "After a letter to [HUD Secretary] Pierce from the conservative Colorado brewer, HUD approved more than $16 million in Denver rent subsidies that had seemed doomed." The Coors family members not only fund the New Right and Religious Right but also are identified by influential Republicans, ranking conservative congressional representatives, and key executive agency appointees as having personal clout in the electoral political arena.

There are other powerful New Right funders. Richard Mellon Scaife, heir to the Mellon fortune, has funneled more than $8 million to the right-wing Free Congress Foundation (FCF) through the Scaife and Carthage Foundations. Other major FCF funders include Robert H. Krieble, retired chairman and honorary director of the Loctite Corporation; Michael and Helen Valerio of the Papa Gino's restaurant chain; and Mr. and Mrs. Roger Milliken of Milliken & Company, makers of the trademarked Visa fabrics, a product featured in full-page, full-color advertisements in John Birch Society publications.

Yet it is the Coors family, primarily Joe, Holly, William, Jeffrey (and Peter at the Coors Foundation), who time and again appear in leadership roles in New Right institutions, offering a guiding hand along with their signed checks. The Coors family's seminal and continuing influence on the politics of the New Right and Religious Right is undeniable. They are among the most powerful bloc of New Right funders and leaders; and are seen as being in the front rank of U.S. conservative power brokers by critics and compatriots alike. With the thawing Cold War melting long-standing alliances among a variety of conservative and right-wing constituencies, the views of the major funders of the largest New Right institutions will to a large degree shape the nature of conservative and reactionary activism in the coming decades. To study the past actions and ideas of the Coors family provides an imperfect yet useful glimpse into the future of the U.S. political Right.

At the same time, the influence of the Heritage Foundation and Free Congress Foundation, both of which represent and reflect the views of the Coors family in Washington, D.C., continues to remain strong. For instance, both institutions helped coordinate the recruitment and selection of conservatives for political appointment by the Bush Administration, and a number of key Bush Administration appointees regularly correspond with and solicit advice from the FCF's Paul Weyrich.

Yet there is another, more subtle reason to study the Coors family. With owners who are such unabashed defenders of an unfettered free enterprise economy, it is understandable that the Coors Corporation would seek to increase profits by promoting the increased sale of its beers to new consumers; and thus Coors has sought to develop new markets among women, African-Americans, Hispanics, gay men, and lesbians. Ironically, the Coors family uses their share of the beer sale profits to promote theories that would roll back the political and social gains made in the past thirty years by persons in these same social groups. The Coors beer label displays a vivid example of this irony—a symbol certifying that Coors is a Kosher product.

Many potential critics of the policies promulgated and promoted by the Coors family members seem mesmerized by the positive images projected in the slick Coors Corporation advertising campaigns. In this report, Mr. Bellant demonstrates the dramatic divergence between Coors corporate imagery and Coors family ideology as reflected by the family's funding of rightist networks. While the Coors Corporation press office tells reporters that Coors family funding of rightists is all in the past, the fact is that these funding patterns are both longstanding and ongoing.

Joe Coors, the ideological leader of the Coors clan, is a latter-day Lone Ranger urging us to return once again to those glorious (if romanticized) days of yesteryear, where men were men and women's role was to deliver their healthy babies; where there was never any doubt as to what was good and what was evil; where minorities had the good sense to live within their God-imposed stereotypes, and godless heathens could be expeditiously dealt with because they had no souls.

There is no question that Joe Coors is motivated by passionate patrio-tism. The question is what price the majority of us in this country will have to pay in order for Joe Coors and his energetic family to realize their backward vision.

Chip Berlet
Cambridge, Massachusetts
7/29/91

*This book is dedicated to the memory of
Amalgamated Clothing & Textile Workers
Union leader Bernie Firestone,
committed to the trade union movement,
peace, civil rights, and social justice.*

ACKNOWLEDGMENTS

BY RUSS BELLANT

M any people helped with the research and publishing of this book. Among them I would especially like to thank Ernesto Vigil, Wes McCune, Chris Takagi, and Ken DeBey. Lou Wolf, David Ivon, Debra Angeline, and members of the Coalition Against English Only were also very helpful. Sara Diamond's research in this field and her book *Spiritual Warfare* have been invaluable. Cable TV reporter "Rick X" provided many useful documents. The *Charleston Gazette* and *Covert Action Information Bulletin* were diligent and courteous in responding to requests for photographs and graphics.

Special thanks to the Funding Exchange for providing funding for the project and to its staff, particularly Paul Smith, for their help.

Political Research Associates director Jean Hardisty gave support and thoughtful comments through many drafts of the manuscript. PRA's Chip Berlet and Margaret Quigley carefully edited the manuscript and spent many hours compiling the extensive index. Quigley also researched the footnotes while Berlet collected the graphics. Susie Chancey helped them with fact-checking.

While this project would not have been possible without the support of the persons and groups named above, and many others who are not named here, I am nonetheless responsible for any errors in the manuscript.

Russ Bellant
Detroit, Michigan
4/18/90

CONTENTS

INTRODUCTION

The Coors empire began in 1873 when German immigrant Adolph Coors set up a brewery in Golden, Colorado. In 1880, when Adolph Coors bought out his partner, it became (and has remained) a family-controlled operation. Adolph Coors, Jr. took over the company in 1929 when his father died after a fall from a Florida hotel window. Whether the father fell or jumped from that ledge is unclear, but the younger Adolph inherited a company which was producing porcelain products, cement, and malted milk. Beer production had been discontinued in 1916, when Colorado voted for statewide Prohibition.[1]

Although Adolph Coors, Sr. came to the United States to avoid the military draft, he was a disciplinarian with others. His grandson, William Coors, remembers him as a "strict taskmaster." Adolph, Jr. was also a harsh disciplinarian who would "wallop the tar out of me and Joe" for childish transgressions, William Coors says of his father.

Joe and William Coors took over the company from their father after his death in 1970. Other family members served as executives and directors of the firm. Over time, two of Joe Coors' five sons, Jeffrey and Peter, were cultivated to take over the primary corporate and political operations of the family empire.

At the end of 1987, Joe Coors announced his semi-retirement and the assumption of CEO tasks by Jeffrey Coors. Other sons, Grover, Adolph Coors IV, Peter, and Joseph Coors, Jr., have run subsidiaries of the Adolph Coors Company. As of early 1990, William Coors is president of the parent corporation, the Adolph Coors Company; Peter Coors is president of Coors Brewing Co.; Jeffrey Coors is president of the Coors Technology Companies; and Joseph Coors, Jr. is president of the Coors Porcelain Company. The entire financial empire is tightly controlled by the family, and while shares of stock are sold to investors, only non-voting shares are issued.

With the ascendancy of the younger Coors management, there is no sign of major changes in the family outlook. In reporting Joe Coors' retirement and the new, younger leadership, the *Denver Post* headline announced "few changes expected." A *Los Angeles Times* profile of the Coors family noted that Peter and Jeffrey, "more than the other brothers. . .bristle with ambition." On the passing over of the eldest son, Joseph, to make Jeffrey and Peter the bosses, the *Times* concluded, "These two are 14–carat chips off the old block, good old boys always, model reflections of the Coors' way of doing and thinking." The Coors' family way of funding and leading the New Right and Religious Right has been passed on to this younger team as well. The younger generation will lead the corporation and its foundation into a new era of political activity, which so far resembles the ways of their forefathers.

The Coors family is a major donor to social, political, and educational charitable projects. With few exceptions, Coors family philanthropy reflects the family's deeply conservative views. Similarly, the personal affiliations of Coors family members (including family memberships in groups and on advisory boards) indicate a coherent Coors family worldview. It is true that the Coors family, foundation, and corporation, through grants and advertising, have expanded their funding in recent years to include groups who historically have not been allies, such as feminist, lesbian and gay, African-American, and Chicano organizations. This shift, however, reflects the family's pragmatic business sense rather than any change in political orientation. Significant funding continues to flow toward rightist groups. The Coors Corporation's public image has been substantially improved through a relatively small investment of time and money.

The involvement of the Coors family with the Heritage Foundation, Free Congress Foundation, and the Council for National Policy provides the family with a conservative political base. From this base, the family is connected to prominent conservative and right-wing activists in other New Right organizations, to groups of the Religious Right, and to allies in government agencies and in Congress. It is natural for conservative activists from a variety of groups to meet and plan strategy and forge alliances. What is surprising is the extent of Coors family involvement with groups which belong properly to neither the New Right nor the Religious Right but to the fringes of the ultra-right, where racists and anti-Semites can be found. Even more disheartening is the extent to which "mainstream" political organizations (many proudly wearing their new-found public respectability garnered through the steady rightward shift in the U.S. political scene during the past decade) evince a willingness to work with these denizens of the fringe.

For the researcher, the magnitude of Coors family philanthropy can be daunting—hundreds of conservative and right-wing groups have been funded by the Coors family. The purpose of this work is to explore some aspects of the Coors family's political involvement, particularly by demonstrating the family's primary role in the establishment and maintenance of key organizations which define the political dialogue for both the New Right and the Religious Right: the Heritage Foundation, the Free Congress Foundation, and the Council for National Policy.

The Coors family is a powerful, wealthy, highly-organized force for social change. The change they support with their time and money is a return to Darwinian political and economic morality framed by the unrestricted demands of market and capital. They also fund a right-wing sector of Christian fundamentalists who seek to replace democratic pluralism with what they call "traditional family values" but which, in fact, is an authoritarian, gender-based social order.

The Coors family supports a *laissez-faire*, free enterprise capitalist system, which sees racism ending with the Civil War and leaving no enduring legacy in the twentieth century. In international affairs, Third World countries are expected to reject alliances with the Soviet Union and to embrace American capital investment without restrictions. The Coors family has given money to groups which supported the white-run apartheid government in South Africa, the violent RENAMO army in Mozambique, and the Pretoria-supported UNITA forces in Angola.

The Coors family funds "pro-family" organizations which advocate maintaining a rigid social order in the midst of a society experiencing rapid change. They support groups which lament the breakdown of what is called the traditional American family, where the mother raises the children and the father earns their living. They say that homosexuals are an abomination and that AIDS is God's judgment on homosexuals. The Coors family funds organizations which believe in Christian, segregated schools. They have supported groups working in alliance with Rev. Sun Myung Moon and Christian Reconstructionists, both of whom have called for the abolition of American democracy and the establishment of a theocratic state.

The Coors family, which in this report refers specifically to Joe, Holly, William, Jeffrey, and Peter Coors, have dedicated personal, corporate, and foundation resources to create a new world. The Coors family shares a deeply felt vision of what America and the world should be with a great many other conservative and right-wing individuals and organizations. This book examines the people and groups who share the Coors family vision—a vision that bears little resemblance to the carefully-crafted corporate image.

THE HERITAGE FOUNDATION

NEW RIGHT IDEOLOGUES

The Heritage Foundation is often characterized as a "conservative think tank," with origins in New Right activism. It is less a traditional think tank, however, than a propaganda center that creates justifications for preconceived positions and then professionally packages the results in a format palatable to politicians and the press. The Heritage Foundation perpetuates what author Alan Crawford calls a "staff ideology." In his benchmark 1980 book *Thunder on the Right*, Crawford noted that Heritage Foundation studies "invariably confirm the notions to which its conservative colleagues and trustees, who include [Joe] Coors, [Coors aide Jack] Wilson, former Reagan aide Frank Walton, California industrialist J. Robert Fluor, are already committed. The founder's real interest. . .appears to be less with balanced public policy research and more with the provision of support for New Right opinions."[2]

"The founder," beer magnate Joe Coors, donated the first-year Heritage budget of $250,000 for 1973 from the coffers of the Coors Corporation.

When Coors, Wilson, and Paul Weyrich began planning a political research entity, they first established Analysis and Research, Inc. in Washington, D.C. on January 15, 1971. For the next two years, Coors gave $200,000 to the group, which failed to attract other supporters. Coors then pledged $15,000 per month in 1973 to the Robert M. Schuchman Foundation, but conflicts arose over Coors' intended use of the tax exempt group. According to author Crawford, the Schuchman board balked at some of

Coors' plans for lobbying and political action—activities that can lead to IRS sanctions against tax exempt groups. Eventually, Coors and Weyrich set up the Committee for the Survival of a Free Congress to carry out political activities and the Heritage Foundation as a tax exempt educational research entity. The Coors company provided Heritage Foundation with $20,000 per month during the foundation's first year. Weyrich was Heritage president until February 28, 1974.[3]

The *Washington Post* says another reason some Schuchman directors felt uneasy about their new allies was Weyrich's ties to Franz Josef Strauss of Bavaria, Germany. Strauss, now deceased, was active in a political party that coalesced with unrepentant Nazis after World War II. According to T. H. Tetens, the British press once referred to Strauss as "the most dangerous man in Europe." As head of the state government of Bavaria, Strauss saw to it that funding was provided to at least one emigré Nazi-collaborationist group, the Organization of Ukrainian Nationalists (OUN).[4]

Weyrich maintained friendly relations with Strauss' Washington representative, Armin K. Haas. When Weyrich was an aide to Senator Gordon Allot, Haas used to send him "mounds of material" attacking the "Ostpolitik" (détente) policies of Chancellor Willy Brandt. Weyrich would write speeches conveying the Haas-Strauss message for Senator Allot and for other Congressmen such as Philip Crane and Edward J. Derwinski. (Derwinski, it was later revealed, had his own leadership role in an ethnic organization peppered with Nazis.)[5] When Strauss came to the United States in the early 1970's, Weyrich and Haas planned his schedule, including Capitol Hill appointments. Joe Coors also helped Haas make new political contacts in Congress.[6]

Weyrich grew up in the German immigrant community of Wisconsin and he continues to reflect the views of certain political tendencies in that ethnic community.[7] Crawford has observed that Paul Weyrich "represents a direct link to the isolationist/populist/Germanophile roots of the New Right." Weyrich says he grew up with great admiration for Robert Taft, a political figure who led the fight against U.S. entry into the war against Hitler's Germany. "I read everything he wrote," Weyrich told Crawford. Crawford noted that Taft only "wrote a short tract on isolationism" and compiled a collection of speeches. Weyrich has also written, "Many of the Catholic New Right activists have a further element in common: their parents were often faithful listeners to radio broadcasts through the 1930's and 1940's of Father Charles Coughlin," who Weyrich simply calls "the noted political commentator." Coughlin could more accurately be described as a demagogic anti-Semite who inspired the zealous Christian Front stormtrooper gangs which attacked Jews in the streets. Father Coughlin militantly opposed any U.S. efforts to hinder Hitler's war efforts, even after the attack on Pearl Harbor. According to Crawford, Coughlin "made direct use of Goebbel's speeches, quoting the Nazi almost word-for-word."[8]

From 1973 to 1982, the chairman of the Heritage Foundation's board of trustees was former Congressman Ben Blackburn, whom *The New York Times* judged in 1975, "not only to be an extreme reactionary but also one whose ideological zeal and lack of judgment made him conspicuous."[9]

Blackburn told a Senate committee that questioned him about his opposition to civil rights that "voting was not an inherent right but a privilege that should be qualified by some sort of literacy test." Blackburn was nominated for a federal appointment by President Gerald Ford in October 1975. The Senate committee interviewing Blackburn asked him about his 1972 testimony before a House committee where he advocated public hanging as an object lesson for public housing tenants who fell behind in their rent payments. The Senate committee rejected Blackburn, who continued to serve as Heritage's chair and would later join the Council for National Policy.[10]

In 1974, Heritage injected itself into a textbook censorship case in Kanawha County, West Virginia when the Kanawha school board approved new textbooks for the school system which included the city of Charleston. The protest was publicly framed as a parents' rights case but, in fact, was focused substantially on books by African-American authors or texts that dealt with the conditions and culture of African-Americans. The Ku Klux Klan was involved in the protest from the start.[11]

According to the sworn testimony of the Reverend James Lewis, who was then pastor of a Charleston Episcopal church, three leading protest leaders were Rev. Marvin Horan, Rev. Ezra Graley, and Ed Miller. Miller was "a self-proclaimed Klansman," according to Lewis. Horan was shown on the steps of the Capitol with robed Klansmen in a Charleston newspaper photo. Horan was also charged with conspiracy to blow up county schools. Graley, who worked in "close concert" with Miller and Horan in rallies and meetings, was the liaison to the Heritage Foundation. Heritage sent staff counsel James T. McKenna to represent the book protesters. Congressman Philip Crane sent out a fundraising appeal for the book protesters. Crane's office refused to tell Lewis, who led an effort to counter the censorship groups, where the funds were going, although Lewis later learned that the letter was part of a Heritage Foundation effort. McKenna complained obliquely to the *Washington Post*, "It's gotten to be that you can't stand up for a minority without being called John Birch, KKK or Nazi."[12]

When Ed Feulner became president of the Heritage Foundation in 1977, Roger Pearson, a person virtually unknown in the United States outside of white supremacist groups and Washington's New Right networks, joined the editorial board of *Policy Review*, the monthly Heritage publication.

Pearson was better known in Europe's racialist networks, where he had been a writer and organizer for the Northern League. The Northern League, peppered with veterans of the Third Reich, was a bizarre pagan Nazi group active in the countries of northern Europe.[13]

Pearson came to the U.S. in 1965 at the invitation of his longtime American ally, Willis Carto, a virulent hate-monger and conspiracist who launched the Institute for Historical Review (IHR) and the Liberty Lobby. IHR denies the Nazi Holocaust against Jews and other targeted groups ever took place, and sponsors conferences where notorious anti-Semites and racists are featured speakers. The quasi-Nazi Liberty Lobby maintains its offices a few blocks from the Capitol where it produces the weekly *Spotlight*, a newspaper which perpetuates the views of Carto by celebrating neo- Nazi skinheads, the Waffen SS, armed anti-Semites, and other anti-democratic forces.

In 1966, Pearson published a series of monographs which expounded his racialist theories, including one that states, "If a nation with a more advanced, more specialized, or in any way superior set of genes mingles with, instead of exterminating, an inferior tribe, then it commits racial suicide." Another monograph was acknowledged to be based on the work of one of Hitler's racial theoreticians, Hans Gunther, who was also a friend of Pearson.[14]

Pearson's tenure on Heritage's *Policy Review* editorial board was short-lived, however, due to a *Washington Post* exposé of the racist and fascist undercurrents at a World Anti-Communist League (WACL) meeting chaired by Pearson in May 1978 in Washington, D.C. The League was the subject of a 1986 book, *Inside the League*, which says the international group was founded and has long been controlled by a core of persons which includes "terrorists, Nazis and Latin American death squad leaders." The *Washington Post* identified Italian fascists and groups with a racist and Nazi character at the WACL meeting, and highlighted Pearson's own racialist background and allies. Pearson chaired the American branch of WACL, the Council on American Affairs, from 1975 to 1980, as well as WACL itself in 1978–79.[15]

The Council on American Affairs (CAA) during the mid-1970's published a number of monographs on international issues and anti-union themes with editors and contributors from the Heritage Foundation. Ed Feulner, for instance, edited a Pearson study sympathetic to the Taiwanese one-party dictatorship in 1976.[16]

Although Pearson's name was dropped from *Policy Review* after the *Washington Post* story, several Heritage leaders joined the editorial advisory board of Pearson's *Journal of Social and Economic Studies*. Stuart M. Butler, director of domestic issues for Heritage, defended his tie to Pearson by claiming that Pearson was not a racist. After a 1985 *Wall Street Journal* article where Pearson defended his past writings and racial attitudes, Butler said he would drop the Pearson tie only if it became embarrassing to Heritage. Butler's name still appears on Pearson's journal. Ernest van den Haag, also on the *Policy Review* editorial board, is on the Advisory Committee of Pearson's *Journal of Social, Political and Economic Studies*. Van den Haag has also expressed views claiming Blacks are intellectually inferior to whites. In 1977 and 1978, the Coors Foundation made contributions to Pearson's Council on American Affairs.[17]

Another project with the Coors-Weyrich-Heritage imprint was the House Republican Study Committee, a network of conservative Republicans whose staff worked on legislative matters.

Weyrich says he was "somewhat involved" in setting up the Study Committee. Heritage trustee Feulner was director of the Study Committee from 1974–1977, and already enjoyed a relationship with Coors. Coors had made Feulner president of the Heritage predecessor, after Coors began funding the Schuchman Foundation. Feulner told the *Washington Post* that he sent Coors information on the Study Committee's activities that might be of interest to him.[18]

When Feulner edited the monograph defending the Taiwanese one-party dictatorship for Roger Pearson in 1976, he arranged for three other House Republican Study Committee staffers to contribute material: Robert Schuettinger, John D. Hoppe, and Nguyen The Loc.

Robert Schuettinger, an associate of Pearson, in 1982 obtained a signed Reagan endorsement of Pearson's work. The letter, on White House stationery, was used by Pearson in fundraising appeals. The Feulner pro-Taiwan monograph was an outgrowth of a pair of Washington, D.C. seminars which emphasized Congressional involvement, including a talk by then-Congressman Edward Derwinski. Derwinski was later picked by President Bush as Secretary of the Department of Veterans Affairs. The pro-Taiwan seminars were co-sponsored by the House Republican Study Committee and by Pearson's Council on American Affairs. Although seeking to influence Congress in a more favorable orientation toward the Taiwanese government, the Taiwan report does not indicate its sponsor, CAA, was at the time the American branch of the World Anti-Communist League (WACL) which itself is led by and receives substantial funding from Taiwan.[19]

Feulner and the House Republican Study Committee also caught the attention of the Fraser Committee, the Congressional committee investigating Korean Central Intelligence Agency (KCIA) activities in the U.S. in the mid-1970's. The report of the investigation noted, "In 1975, Ed Feulner . . .was introduced to KCIA station chief Kim Yung Hwan by Neil Salonen and Dan Fefferman of the Freedom Leadership Foundation." Salonen was head of Rev. Sun Myung Moon's Unification Church in the United States. The Freedom Leadership Foundation (FLF), a political arm of Moon's Unification network, was linked to the World Anti-Communist League (WACL). The FLF was described as "an organization to be used to achieve KCIA objectives," by the Congressional report, which was based on a KCIA document that discussed FLF.[20]

The report does not indicate what relationship Moon's Unification network had with Feulner that would result in a KCIA introduction, but such links appear to have continued into the 1980's. The former head of South Korean intelligence, Chang Se Tong, testified before the Korean legislature in 1988 that Korean intelligence made a donation to Heritage in the early 1980's. In 1982, Heritage established an Asian Studies Center, which *The Nation* magazine notes "has quartered apologists for Chun's regime [Chun Doo Hwan, the South Korean Prime Minister] ." A list of 1985 donors to Heritage (released by Coors to show that other corporations also support Heritage) includes support from a "Federation of Korean Industries." The Korean legislature, which was investigating corruption in Korea, found a document indicating that the amount donated came to $2.2 million. According to *The Nation*, Heritage failed to report this foreign contribution to the Justice Department as required by law.[21]

The first fellow of the Asian Studies Center was South Korean General Huh Wha Pying, a former director of South Korean military intelligence and one of Chun Doo Hwan's closest advisers. The Asian Studies Center published several cheerleading "Backgrounders" such as "Chun's visit marks South Korea's new ties with the U.S."; "South Korea's Defense Industry: An Asset for the U.S."; and "How a Booming South Korea Exports Jobs to the U.S."[22]

Heritage's Director of Administration in 1980 was Michael Warder, who was a key leader of Moon's Unification network in the United States. Warder was listed as a director of the Unification Church of America in 1977, as well as a director of several state affiliates. He was also secretary to the board of the International Cultural Foundation, an international umbrella organization coordinating a variety of Moon projects. Perhaps the key indicator of Moon's trust of Warder was the fact that in the 1970's Warder was the largest American stockholder in Tong Il Enterprises, the U.S. branch of the Korean-based Moon business empire. Tong Il manufactures M-16's and other weapons, heavy machinery, and parts for the auto and truck industry. Tong Il also is involved in the tuna fishing industry.

A 1978 report of International Oceanic Enterprises, another Moon company, also listed Warder as director. Warder held an editorial position with Moon's News World Communications, Inc., which publishes daily newspapers. Warder claimed in 1981 that he had left the Moon organization but

Right:
Although praised by Weyrich, Father Coughlin gave speeches and wrote tracts with anti-Jewish themes. This pamphlet spun a tale about sinister Jewish conspiracies by "international bankers," and had other clearly anti-Semitic references.
©1938, REV. CHAS. E. COUGHLIN.

Below:
When the Heritage Foundation sent an adviser to help the Kanawha County school textbook protest movement, it joined a political coalition that included the Ku Klux Klan. Here the Klan demonstrates on the steps of the West Virginia State Capitol in support of the textbook protest.
©1975, *CHARLESTON GAZETTE.*

"Unregulated Debts"

By
Rev. Chas. E. Coughlin

Sunday, January 30, 1938

Royal Oak, Mich.

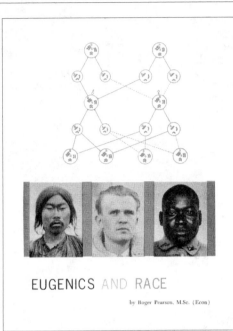

EUGENICS AND RACE

by Roger Pearson, M.Sc. (Econ)

Dr. Roger Pearson's racialist theories are circulated worldwide by neo-Nazi and white supremacist organizations. This edition was published by Noontide Press, which specializes in racialist and eugenicist titles.

©1966, THE NOONTIDE PRESS, ROGER PEARSON.

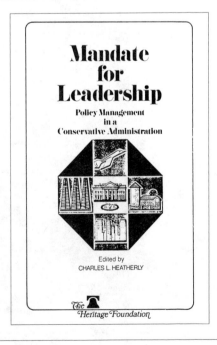

Mandate for Leadership

Policy Management in a Conservative Administration

Edited by
CHARLES L. HEATHERLY

The Heritage Foundation

This Heritage Foundation publication became an unofficial handbook for the incoming Reagan Administration.

©1981, BOARD OF TRUSTEES OF THE HERITAGE FOUNDATION

refused to say anything critical of Moon's Unification network or even discuss the operations with which he was involved. At first, former members of Moon's cult raised the possibility that Warder was following a Moon practice of infiltrating positions of influence. However, nine years after he left, Warder began writing critically of Moon's Unification network. In one article, Warder called the Moon organization "totalitarian" and said, "Ronald Reagan and Walter Mondale have more in common with each other than with Moon. . . Moon's religious and political views are repugnant to conservatism." Warder, however, has not as yet revealed information about the inner workings of the Moon network.[23]

Christian Voice is one Moon-connected group that has operated out of the Heritage building. A "former" Moon operative, Gary Jarmin, attacked critics of Moon and gave an interview to a Moon-controlled newspaper after he joined the Christian Voice (CV) staff. CV's chair, Robert Grant, has been a leader of Moon's Unification network front groups such as the American Freedom Coalition, which fundraised for Oliver North. Jarmin also had a consulting business in the Heritage offices.[24]

According to one knowledgeable conservative source, Heritage has seen itself as a political ally of Moon's but had disagreements with Moon leaders several years ago over the editorship of the Moon-controlled daily, the *Washington Times*. Apparently Heritage wanted Pat Buchanan to become editor, but the paper renewed Arnaud de Borchgrave's contract. Moon has also cut funding to American groups which he supported generously in the past. In June 1989, Feulner criticized direct-mail fundraiser Richard Viguerie for his links to Moon. The relationship between the Heritage/ Coors family circles and the Moon network are significant both because Moon's Unification Church uses cultist, emotionally-manipulative organizing techniques, and because Moon has openly called for an end to democracy in the United States. Also, the Fraser Committee found the Moon operations to be interwoven with KCIA activities and, since the 1961 South Korean coup, a component of support for the military dictatorship there.[25]

The Heritage Foundation is best known for its production of tomes that compile recommendations for altering or abolishing government policies and agencies. In 1980, Heritage published *Mandate for Leadership* to guide the incoming Reagan Administration and its transition team. The several thousand recommendations called for more money and latitude for the Pentagon and intelligence agencies, with reductions and restrictions on spending for education, welfare, health, and other social services. A number of the authors of the report and other Heritage people were later hired by the Reagan Administration to implement their recommended policies.[26]

Working the high-level inside track on these personnel hirings was Reagan's "Kitchen Cabinet," of which Joe Coors was probably the best-known member. A Reagan loyalist since the 1968 GOP convention, Coors began spending a lot of time in Washington, D.C. and the White House. The attempt at governance by the Kitchen Cabinet became so elaborate that they actually established an office in the Executive Office Building across from the White House. Embarrassed by the image of a covey of millionaires seeming to run parallel and sometimes conflicting personnel recruitment operations, senior White House staff produced legal opinions saying that it was illegal for a private group to occupy government property, in this case a White House office. Although Coors produced a legal opinion arguing there was no violation of law, Coors and friends were evicted.[27]

Heritage could hardly claim diminished relations with the Reagan Administration, however, as an estimated two-thirds of its *Mandate* recommendations were adopted in the first year of the Administration. Further, Heritage was using a letter of endorsement from White House Chief of Staff Ed Meese in a December 1981 fundraising effort. In his letter of endorsement, Meese promised Feulner that "this Administration will cooperate fully with your efforts." After leaving the Reagan Administration, Meese joined the staff of the Heritage Foundation. The Heritage Foundation told potential donors that a contribution of $1,000 or more to the Foundation would entitle the donor to meet with top White House officials.[28]

Conflict did arise once between the Pentagon and Heritage when a 1983 Heritage report included criticism of certain weapons programs and military procurement and planning procedures. Heritage promoted this critique until Secretary of Defense Caspar Weinberger saw it. The four military branches were ordered by him to write separate rebuttals. Navy Secretary John Lehman sent the Navy's rebuttal not to Heritage, but to Joe Coors. Coors called Feulner, and the public relations blitz for the critique stopped "instantly," according to an *Atlantic Monthly* account of the events.

Since Lehman knew Feulner from their days as roommates at Georgetown College, and since Feulner had once been a "confidential assistant" to Melvin Laird when Laird was Secretary of Defense, Lehman could have sent his critique directly to Heritage where it would have reached an acquaintance familiar with Pentagon matters. Lehman's decision to send his memo to Joe Coors indicated that Coors was, in 1983, still the key power behind Heritage despite its diversified funding. So complete was Heritage's reversal that the report's author, George Kuhn, "was given the silent treatment, and received no further Heritage work," according to the *Atlantic Monthly*. References to Kuhn's work disappeared even though Heritage normally promotes reports as long as six years after their initial publication.[29]

When Reagan was reelected in 1984, Heritage published a sequel, *Mandate for Leadership II*, that called for cutbacks in or elimination of

programs which provided food stamps, Medicare, child nutrition, farm assistance, and legal services for the poor, and the repeal of a $1,000 tax
exemption for the elderly. It advocated a "top priority" fight against comparable worth; the expansion of so-called "low-intensity" warfare in nine
Third World countries; and policy processes that would in effect keep civil
service employees from knowing the real policy goals of political appointees
in federal agencies.[30]

The authors of the Heritage *Mandate for Leadership II* section on education advocated turning the Department of Education into a "three-room
school house." The report's author, Eileen Gardner, was later forced to
resign as a consultant to the Department of Education when she defended
her 1983 draft of a Heritage report which stated, "Laws for the education of
the handicapped, then, have selfishly drained resources from the normal
school population. . . .In a misguided effort to help a few, the many have
been injured." Elsewhere in the report, Gardner made a rather disturbing
justification for her cruel attitudes toward the handicapped: "There is no
injustice in the universe. As unfair as it may seem, a person's external
circumstances fit his level of inner spiritual development." She also claimed
that handicapped people have "summoned" their own problems. After her
resignation, Gardner returned to the Heritage Foundation.[31]

In what can justifiably be described as a blueprint for extending domestic
racial discrimination and political repression, Heritage also recommended
that the Justice Department limit voting rights enforcement, end federal
support for set-aside programs for minority contractors, and reinstate an
order requiring that more than 100,000 federal officials submit, for the rest
of their lives, advance copies of their speeches and writings to be censored.
Heritage also called for a federal death penalty, reduced penalties for price-
fixers and antitrust violators, and stepped-up pornography prosecutions.
These recommendations for the Justice Department were written for the
Heritage Foundation by Paul D. Kamenar, executive legal director of the
Washington Legal Foundation, which has enjoyed more than a decade of
Coors financial support. [32]

The 1984 proposal for so-called "low-intensity" warfare in nine countries
was a recommendation for ongoing covert paramilitary warfare to enforce
the premise that "the U.S. no longer will countenance the subversion or
overthrow of friendly governments within the developing world." The
report said that in targeted countries, "Indigenous operational assets can be
identified and developed, and the staff resources of the Central Intelligence
Agency and DOD are in a position to expand significantly if required for a
joint operational effort." This proposal carries with it the possibility of
eventual direct U.S. military intervention to control uncooperative countries. The report called for "a stronger public consensus than exists today" to

Slava Stetsko addresses a 1989 meeting co-sponsored by the Heritage Foundation and the pro-Nazi Anti-Bolshevik Bloc of Nations. Slava Stetsko heads the ABN and is the widow of Yaroslav Stetsko, leader of the Nazi puppet government in the Ukraine during World War II.

ABN CORRESPONDENCE, THE BULLETIN OF THE ANTI-BOLSHEVIK BLOC OF NATIONS, MAY-JUNE 1989

This second major Heritage Foundation policy publication designed to influence the Reagan Administration proposed gutting federal programs aimed at eliminating racial discrimination and called for cutbacks in or elimination of programs which provided food stamps, Medicare, child nutrition, farm assistance, and legal services for the poor. The report called for extending the use of covert operations in Third World countries.

©1984, THE HERITAGE FOUNDATION.

support such efforts. As Leonard Larsen of the *Denver Post* noted, Heritage would "urge the new policy of violence and point out on the map where it could be employed. . . .Other warriors can be hired or conscripted to do the fighting." The proposal, written by Richard Shultz of the Coors-supported National Strategy Information Center, was nearly identical to the proposal that Maj. Gen. John "Jack" Singlaub, USA (ret.) was quietly championing at the behest of the Reagan Administration several months earlier at the 1984 World Anti-Communist League meeting in San Diego.

The Heritage Foundation generated extensive press coverage to build support for its policy recommendations. Within months of these events, the Reagan Administration was involved in aiding the UNITA rebels against the Angolan government and increasing aid to Afghan rightists. Congress has barely challenged and certainly not reversed these hard-line foreign policy decisions which continue to shape U.S. diplomatic initiatives especially in Africa, Asia, and Central America.[33]

Heritage has produced a vast collection of materials on behalf of business interests in areas of deregulation, environment, taxation, antitrust law, and the trade and industrial unions. In 1987, Heritage had a staff of 135, using a $14.2 million budget to study, educate, advocate, network, and, in the words of a Heritage officer, "do battle." Its proposals go out to over 7,000 Congressional and Administration officials and staff, journalists, and major donors.[34] Reagan's early reputation as a strong, decisive leader, his chief legislative successes with Congress, and his reorganizations of the executive branch were primarily due to the fact that his script had already been written for him by the Heritage Foundation before he won the election.

The Heritage Foundation board of directors has long been dominated by businessmen rather than serious academics. For all the pro-business proposals and propaganda for aiding the empowerment of a pro-business Administration, the businessmen who oversee Heritage get more than their money's worth. As *Atlantic Monthly* noted, a perception of detachment is associated with think tanks, and so they are taken more seriously on Capitol Hill than corporate vice-presidents. *Atlantic Monthly* also notes, "The beauty of it all was that thinkers come cheaper than lobbyists." [35]

The Coors Foundation has given hundreds of thousands of dollars to the Heritage Foundation. The corporation has given large amounts (the $250,000 start-up money in 1973, for instance), as have individual Coors family members. Joe Coors, for instance, helped with the acquisition of Heritage headquarters.

With common sources of funding and board-of-director interlocks with the Free Congress Foundation and Council for National Policy, the Heritage Foundation will continue to be a key element in the phalanx of rightist groups with an agenda of austerity for the poor, hostility to minorities and women, upward distribution of wealth for the rich, economic domination of the Third World, with repression and bloodletting for those who rebel.

Critical Issues Series

Secular Humanism and the Schools:

The Issue Whose Time Has Come

Onalee McGraw

The
Heritage Foundation
513 C Street, N.E. • Washington, D.C. 20002

Is "Humanism Education" Unconstitutional?

Inasmuch as humanistic curriculum programs and "values-clarification" and "moral-education" teaching strategies are based upon materialistic values found only in man's nature itself, they reject the spiritual and moral tradition of theistic faith and religion. Thus, many parents who subscribe to Judeo-Christian belief oppose humanistic education in the tax-supported schools on grounds that such programs promote and advocate the religion of secular humanism in violation of the First Amendment to the U.S. Constitution.[20]

THE FREE CONGRESS FOUNDATION

"We are no longer working to preserve the status quo.
We are working to overturn the present power
structure in this country . . . ."

Paul Weyrich

RESHAPING AMERICA

One of the key New Right organizations committed to a full range of domestic and foreign policy issues is the Free Congress Foundation, headed by Paul Weyrich. Like the Heritage Foundation, the Free Congress Foundation was started with seed money from the Coors family.[36]

The Free Congress Foundation (FCF) engages in political activity through publishing, organizing forums on Capitol Hill and elsewhere, networking with other right-wing groups, lobbying, and through a related political action committee, Free Congress PAC.

The FCF evolved out of the Committee for the Survival of a Free Congress, established by Weyrich and Joe Coors in July 1974. It has been run by Weyrich ever since, with funding and oversight from the Coors family.

Coors met Weyrich in the early 1970's when Weyrich was press aide for Senator Gordon Allot of Colorado. Their early relationship was described in Alan Crawford's *Thunder on the Right:* "As his (Coors') unofficial agent in the capitol, Weyrich convinced Coors to underwrite the Heritage Foundation and the Committee for the Survival of a Free Congress. He installed himself as a paid employee of both organizations."[37]

Coors began his involvement in national politics in 1971 by sending aide Jack Wilson to Washington to size up projects that Coors might support. Wilson, as one might expect, shared Coors' rightist views. In a 1973 memo to Coors, Wilson stated that "Martin Luther King was an avowed communist revolutionary."[38]

From 1971 to 1974, Coors contributed several hundred thousand dollars to organizations which did not produce the effectiveness that Coors and Weyrich sought. They then set up the Heritage Foundation, and Weyrich was its president for the first year.

Seeking a mechanism to engage directly in electoral politics at the height of the Watergate scandal, Weyrich's Committee for the Survival of a Free Congress rapidly injected itself into the 1974 elections, raising $421,248 and distributing $194,000 to candidates.[39]

From the very beginning, the Committee for the Survival of a Free Congress (CSFC) got involved in local elections, recruiting right-wing candidates as well as supporting announced candidates. Those seeking CSFC support were required to "attend a three-day training seminar to learn a prescribed precinct organization method. Candidates for the House must adopt this method before they can get any funds from CSFC."[40] Those candidates who submitted to the CSFC would also receive polling services and other campaign tools. Since CSFC worked for challengers rather than incumbents, it could be expected that successful candidates would enter the Congress with a certain dependence on CSFC for reelection.

In the 1970's, Richard Viguerie did the direct-mail fundraising for CSFC. At the time he was considered the top fundraiser in the country, scaring up tens of millions of dollars for candidates and causes. Viguerie was also able to impose conditions on candidates so that they became indebted to the New Right machine. Viguerie, along with Paul Weyrich and the late Terry Dolan of the National Conservative Political Action Committee (NCPAC), worked closely on campaigns and issues designed to make themselves national power brokers. One observer of this process wrote in the *Atlantic*: "Viguerie has the whole piece of cake. . . .You can't tell Viguerie what to do. He is the master of his ship and, if you're going to tie your dinghy to it, you go where he goes."[41]

Weyrich, Viguerie, and Howard Phillips, founder of the Conservative Caucus, were trying to create a new center of political action to the right of the Republican Party, which they saw as too moderate. To that end Weyrich, Viguerie, Phillips, and William Rusher went to the 1976 convention of the American Independent Party (AIP) to seek a spot for Viguerie on the national ticket. The AIP, formed as a vehicle for the George Wallace campaign of 1968, was a coalition that included elements of the Ku Klux Klan, John Birchers who declined to move back into the GOP to work for Reagan in the 1976 primaries, and operatives of the Liberty Lobby. As the New Rightists worked the convention floor, the convention's keynote speaker declaimed, to thunderous applause, on the dangers of "atheistic political Zionism (the most insidious, far-reaching murderous force the world has ever known)."[42]

Although Viguerie promised the AIP fundraising benefits from his mailing lists, the convention chose Lester Maddox to head the ticket. Maddox was the white supremacist who gained national notoriety in the early 1960's for threatening African-Americans with ax handles if they attempted to patronize his whites-only restaurant in Georgia.[43]

The conservative weekly *Human Events* reported that the long-range plan of Viguerie, Weyrich, and Phillips was to use the AIP to form the backbone for a new party in the 1980 elections. Rather than rejecting the segregationist AIP, they sought to incorporate the AIP, with its racist, anti-Semitic, and neo-fascist elements, into their plans to shape the future political course of the United States.[44]

Viguerie wasn't the only source of funds for Weyrich during this period. During the 1977–78 election cycle, the Coors family continued to fund Weyrich, giving at least $22,600 to CSFC, according to federal records. Jeffrey, Peter, Joe, and Holly Coors personally donated. Other executives of the Coors company also gave money to Weyrich. The CSFC was advocating anti-gay and lesbian and anti-labor politics in a demagogic manner. In 1977, it advocated a cutoff of federal Legal Services Corporation assistance in legal disputes involving lesbian and gay civil rights. The same year, it also backed legislation limiting federal employee unions and pushed for the defeat of the common site picketing bill supported by the AFL-CIO. Members of the Congress who opposed the CSFC were dubbed "radicals." In what must have been a surprise to many political observers, 137 members of Congress were so labeled, including Claude Pepper (D-FL), Thomas Foley (D-WA), and Les Aspin (D-WI). [45]

Weyrich, Viguerie, Phillips, and several others were involved in setting up many New Right organizations to shape issues, raise money, and put more political power in their hands. One of those groups was the Moral Majority. In her book *Spiritual Warfare: The Politics of the Christian Right*, author Sara Diamond summarizes the events that led to the rise of Jerry Falwell:

> In May 1979, Robert Billings of the National Christian Action Coalition invited Falwell to a meeting with Phillips, Viguerie, Weyrich and Ed McAteer. The four told Falwell of their shared opposition to legalized abortion and pornography, and their

intention to influence the 1980 GOP platform. Weyrich proposed that if the Republican Party could be persuaded to take a firm stance against abortion, that would split the strong Catholic voting block within the Democratic Party. The New Right leaders wanted Falwell to spearhead a visibly Christian organization that would apply pressure to the GOP. Weyrich proposed that the name have something to do with a moral majority.[46]

The group helped Falwell put together a board of directors. Robert Billings, who was also a director of the Free Congress Foundation, became executive director of Moral Majority. Together they led campaigns to abolish sex education, abortion rights, and legal protections for lesbians and gay men. Falwell pledged to "turn this (country) into a Christian nation." During this period, in 1979 and 1980, the Coors family, including Jeffrey, Peter, Joe, and Holly, gave CSFC $31,000, according to Federal Election Commission records. Joe Coors also built the headquarters building for Weyrich's groups. A wing of the building is named for Coors.[47]

The FCF appears to have established ties to elements of the Religious Right more extreme than Moral Majority. Primarily through staffers Connaught (Connie) and William Marshner, the FCF has been represented at meetings of "shepherding discipleship" groups, such as the Ann Arbor-based Word of God.[48]

Shepherding discipleship is a practice begun by some fundamentalist and evangelical religious groups in the 1970's that requires initiates and members to "submit" themselves totally to Christ by placing their lives under the control of a "shepherd." One's personal life, choices of recreation, choices of spouse, weekly schedule of activity, and other matters must be approved by an appointed shepherd.

Word of God (WOG) members are told that leaders have received prophecies directly from God; that they, as members of the Word of God, have been specially chosen to lead God's forces in the coming apocalypse. It is the disciplining process they feel is necessary to pursue this task that leaders say justifies their intimate control of members' lives. A hostile view of the modern secular world is promoted, along with a passion for internal secrecy about the aims and purposes of the group. In 1981, privileged members pledged their willingness to sacrifice their lives and loyalty "to our commanders," referring to WOG leaders. They also pledged to "keep our plans and movements hidden from the enemy and his agents." Members who show signs of independence can be subjected to rites to drive satanic possession from their souls by WOG-appointed exorcists. Former members call the Word of God a cult.[49]

Connie Marshner has participated for years in activities of the Word of God, primarily through a group controlled by WOG called Allies for Renewal. Marshner participated in the Allies for Renewal annual conference in June 1989 which was dominated by WOG speakers.[50]

William Marshner, husband of Connie, considers his exposure to the Word of God one of four positive revelations in his life. He co-authored *Cultural Conservatism*, a FCF book, and teaches at Christendom College in Virginia. He is also one of FCF's senior staff.

Another shepherding network with which Connie Marshner is involved is run by Dennis Peacocke, who directs several groups from his Santa Rosa, California headquarters. One group is the Coalition on Revival (COR), which sought to recruit pastors to establish shepherding techniques in their churches. While national in scope, COR is focusing on a ten-year plan to take over the county governments of conservative Orange County and Santa Clara County (Silicon Valley) in California. Connie Marshner is on the steering committee and Peacocke is secretary to COR, which advocates a "muscular" form of Christianity which "takes theology to the streets." COR has developed detailed plans for taking over government, law, education, media, economics, and entertainment in the U.S. and Canada. It represents a key umbrella of various shepherding leaders and far-right activists.[51]

Peacocke himself is a shepherd over Colonel Doner, director of Christian Voice, one of the key Christian rightist groups working to elect conservative Republicans. Robert Grant, chairman of Christian Voice, is very active within the Reverend Sun Myung Moon's Unification Church network's political operations. Peacocke in turn is submitted to Bob Mumford, one of the foremost shepherding leaders in the U.S. and a key ally of the Word of God for fifteen years. Mumford and WOG leaders formed a group in 1974 to plan "national and world strategies."[52]

Another group, the secretive Anatole Fellowship, was founded by Peacocke to "gain influence within the Republican Party" on behalf of the Religious Right. Marshner serves on the executive committee of Anatole. One 1987 meeting in Washington, D.C. was arranged in which "Weyrich's Free Congress Foundation was a key player in the two-day meeting, which focused on issues ranging from school-based health clinics to 1988 electoral strategies to South Africa, Nicaragua and El Salvador," according to Sara Diamond's *Spiritual Warfare*.[53]

An undated Anatole letter to state-level coalition members advised:

> For Christians to be successful in influencing legislation in Washington, D.C., it is imperative that we have a national communications network to inform God's people of issues of concern to them. To this end the Anatole Fellowship has

formed an issues committee co-chaired by Connie Marshner and Peter Waldron. For communication purposes Connie Marshner has been selected to write a monthly legislative alert. Because an effort is being made to keep the Anatole Fellowship as low-profile as possible, Connie is writing on the letterhead of her organization. . . .

Our success in Washington will largely be determined by our ability to generate letters and phone calls on the key issues. Our effectiveness in doing this depends on your sharing the contents of these 'alerts' with the Christian activist organizations in your state and mobilizing them behind these issues.[54]

Pete Waldron is also a member of the Council for National Policy and the steering committee of Coalition on Revival.

Another undated *Anatole Alert* directed associates to support Jonas Savimbi's UNITA, a military force supported financially by South Africa and allied operationally with South Africa's military campaign to destabilize Angola and strategically control the southern portion of Africa. The Anatole newsletter also counseled against Senate ratification of the Genocide Treaty, an international pact which criminalizes genocidal actions. Peacocke was also active in recruiting and training anti-Sandinista religious leaders in Central America.[55]

Marshner not only serves on Peacocke's boards, but Peacocke serves on the board of Marshner's National Pro-Family Coalition, which operates out of Free Congress Foundation offices. Also on Marshner's board is Roy Jones of Moral Majority and former Michigan Congressman Mark Siljander, a member of COR's steering committee. While in Congress, he was a "sheep" submitted to an aide who was actually his shepherd, according to three other Siljander aides. A February 1986 letter of the "pro-family" group also urged support of Savimbi and opposition to the genocide treaty.[56]

An anti-choice group, American Coalition for Life, also lists Connie Marshner, Peacocke, Jones, Tim LaHaye (a leader of Moral Majority and founder of the Council for National Policy), Siljander, Gary North (a prominent Christian Reconstructionist), and Herb Titus (head of Pat Robertson's Regent University—formerly CBN University) on its letterhead. The Coalition trains their workers at Morton Blackwell's Leadership Institute. (*See the section on CNP*)

Another component of the Coalition on Revival supported by Coors is the National Association of Christian Educators (NACE) of Costa Mesa, California. Headed by Robert L. Simonds of the COR steering committee, NACE sent out a letter in June 1989 outlining its work with COR. The letter begins "Beloved Christian Warrior" and discusses NACE's role in implementing COR's plan in the field of education, one of seventeen spheres of social life COR delineates. The five-year plan calls for rallies, banquets, the formation of new organizations and eventually taking over school boards "to redeem your great city's children from atheist and immoral domination," and to "reclaim our Christian heritage in our public schools." The COR plan targets sixty cities in its first phase. The Coors Foundation gave NACE $47,000 from 1985 to 1988.[57]

While the interconnections of COR and political activity are complex, the end goals are not. COR has been heavily influenced by the reactionary Christian Reconstruction movement; both R.J. Rushdoony and Gary North serve on COR's steering committee. The Christian Reconstructionists would replace the U.S. Constitution with their literal interpretation of biblical law and would adopt, for example, the Old Testament's draconian provisions for capital punishment. (*See the section on the Council for National Policy for further information on the Christian Reconstructionists*) Like the Christian Reconstructionists, the Coalition on Revival's leaders seek an end to democracy and the imposition of a Christian republic that in fact is totalitarian, ruling all dimensions of societal life.[58]

Marshner and her husband, William, recently resigned in protest from the Editorial Advisory Board of *Fidelity* after the conservative Catholic magazine published a critique of the "anti-democratic" Society for the Defense of Tradition, Family and Property (TFP) and made reference to "hundreds of articles accusing the TFP of 'having Nazi-Fascist tendencies.' " *Fidelity* noted that the Marshners (and others who had complained about the article, including Michael Schwartz and Enrique Rueda) were employees or associates of Paul Weyrich, president of the Coors-supported Free Congress Foundation and a staunch defender of the TFP. [59]

The TFP co-sponsored a December 1989 Conservative Leadership Conference initiated by Weyrich, Blackwell, and Reed Irvine. Other co-sponsors included the Moon network's political organizing arm, American Freedom Coalition, the National Right to Life Committee, and the Republican National Committee. Attendees heard White House drug policy adviser William Bennett joke about public beheadings of drug sellers as a means to deter drug use.[60]

The Free Congress Foundation is generally identified with the "secular" New Right rather than the "Religious" New Right, but, in fact, it melds both currents of rightist activity. Although structurally one organization, FCF could be seen as a dozen semi-independent groups housed in one office complex and with one boss.

The FCF divides many of its activities into "Centers." There are centers for Government and Politics; Law and Democracy; Cultural Conservatism; State Policy; Conservative Governance; Child and Family

Policy; Foreign Policy; Transportation Policy; and Catholic Policy.

In the FCF's 1988 Annual Report, the Center for Catholic Policy states, "The public policy influence and activity of the Catholic Church in America often runs counter to the interests of Catholic laity. The Center for Catholic Policy seeks to instruct conservative Catholic laity how to become influential in shaping public policy stands taken by the Church." The FCF report says that a "network of some forty national Catholic organizations, institutions and publications which share a generally conservative viewpoint" was formed by FCF in January 1988, and called the Siena Group.[61]

According to the FCF:

> Among the top priorities of the Siena Group in 1988 was mobilizing opposition to a U.S. Catholic Conference statement on AIDS policy which was favorable to the objectives of the gay and lesbian rights movement. Siena Group participants convinced the bishops to set aside the AIDS document. . .[62]

The Siena Group's long-range plans include "promoting orthodoxy in Catholic parochial schools and universities; gaining more visible support for pro-family social policies from official Catholic agencies; and supporting religious freedom, particularly in Central America and the Soviet bloc."[63] The meeting that spawned the Siena Group was hosted by Tom Monaghan, chairman of Domino's Pizza, who called the event historically "important," and one which he hoped would lead to an "authentic renewal of the Church *and society*" (author's emphasis). Monaghan is a founder of a Catholic businessmen's group called Legatus. Both Monaghan and Legatus are involved with and interact with the Word of God shepherding group. At least one Legatus meeting had speakers from FCF, including Weyrich. According to one source, Legatus and a Word of God front group known as the Center for Pastoral Renewal, are members of the Siena Group.[64]

Foreign policy initiatives at the Free Congress Foundation are represented by two elements, the Center for Foreign Policy and the *Freedom Fighter* newsletter.

The Center for Foreign Policy was established in April 1986 under the direction of William Kling, a former director of the Washington office of the American Security Council. In concert with Weyrich's International Policy Forum, the center has conducted political training for right-wing leaders from around the world. It has been especially active in Chile where Augusto Pinochet's military dictatorship was under intense international criticism for several years. In 1987, FCF wrote that they had "contributed a balanced perspective and essential new information much needed in volatile public discussions over Chile's efforts—in the face of Marxist terrorism and violence—to reestablish democratic government. . ." The FCF says that

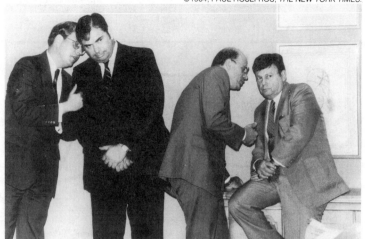

(Left to right): **Paul Weyrich of the Free Congress Foundation, Howard Phillips of the Conservative Caucus, New Right direct-mail specialist Richard Viguerie, and Max Hugel, former deputy director of the CIA. The photograph of the four key New Right strategists was taken as they conferred while at the 1984 Republican convention. Their attempts to push the platform at the 1984 Republican convention far to the right were chronicled in *The New York Times Magazine.***

Paul Weyrich of the Free Congress Foundation has long represented Coors family interests in Washington, D.C. A reactionary rightist, Weyrich pushes an anti-democratic and authoritarian agenda. Weyrich's associates Connie and William Marshner resigned from the board of the conservative Catholic magazine *Fidelity* when the magazine said the Society for the Defense of Tradition, Family and Property (TFP), a group Weyrich supports, was "anti-democratic" and quoted critics who charged that TFP had "Nazi-Fascist tendencies."

COUNCIL FOR NATIONAL POLICY, MEETING PROGRAM, FEBRUARY 1989, ORLANDO, FLORIDA.

VOL. III, NO. 11   *The monthly report of the Freedom League and the Freedom Research Foundation*   MAY 1988

The Reagan Doctrine: Victory And Defeat

In the final months of the Reagan Administration, an assessment is coming in to focus. Afghanistan is the Reagan Administration's great achievement. Nicaragua is its great failure. The Soviets are about to retreat from Afghanistan in a rout, under full-scale attack by the *mujahideen*. This should have been the fate of the Sandinistas at the hands of the Contras.

That it is not is the fault of two men: Ronald Reagan and Jim Wright. All Jim Wright can talk about, it seems, is "peace." We now know how Jim Wright spells peace: SURRENDER.   At the crucial junction, when the Contras were at their strongest—increasing in military strength, taking the battle to the Communist foe—and the Sandinistas at their weakest—their military morale collapsing, facing riots and protests in the streets, and their economy bankrupt with 1000 percent inflation— Jim Wright snatched defeat from the jaws of victory. So great is his lust for power, so great is his indifference to the security of his country, so great is his hatred for Ronald Reagan, that he, with malice aforethought, secured the surrender of the Nicaraguan freedom fighters and sold out Nicaragua to the Soviet Union.

Now the march to a Soviet Central America has begun. Within days of the Contras' sell out, Daniel Ortega threatened to annihilate them militarily, and our consulate was burned down in Honduras. We can be assured now that a Marxist insurgency will shortly arise in Honduras as that former ally of ours swings sharply anti-American and to the left. Jim Wright will see to it that the newly-elected forces of D'Abuisson in El Salvador receive no aid, so that it too will go the down the Communist tube. The only remaining stepping stone to Mexico will be Guatemala, already under Communist siege.

Ronald Reagan permitted this to happen. Over and over again he has voiced his support for the Contras, yet he allowed them to be sold out by Jim Wright. And his State Department would have sold out the *mujahideen* if the Senate had not prevented it.

The lesson is that the Reagan Doctrine succeeds when we have the resolve, and fails when we do not. If Congress had supported the Contras as it has the *mujahideen*, the Sandinistas would have been history by now. Because of Congress' unswerving support of the *mujahideen*, the Soviets are soon to be history in Afghanistan.

Due to their quite justifiable suspicion of the State Department, certain conservatives are refusing to admit victory in Afghanistan. It is time to proclaim it, to celebrate it, and capitalize on it.   It is time to see that the Soviets have lost. The families of Soviet officers and advisors at the Shindand Air Base and in Herat and Kabul are flying back to Russia. The oil pipeline from Herat to Shindand is being dismantled. The Soviets' retreat will be bloody. The *mujahideen* have received the message from their commanders: "This is your last chance to become a *Jhazi* (someone who has killed an atheist in a holy war), so kill as many *Shuravi* (Soviets) as you can; teach the *Shuravi* the lesson that they should never even think of coming to Afghanistan ever again." The *mujahideen* are overjoyed that the Soviets are massively supplying their puppets in Kabul: all the more weapons for them to capture, and then turn over to the Moslems in Soviet Central Asia. The Afghans want the Russians to be as far away from them as possible, so they intend to incite a *Jihad* (holy war) to liberate Soviet Moslems from Moscow.

Since liberalism is a form of political masochism, liberals only hate those who are allies of America. The Christian Contras are our friends and allies in a way the

The *Freedom Fighter* magazine glorifies right-wing military forces around the world and claims that "liberals only hate those who are allies of America."

THE FREEDOM FIGHTER, THE MONTHLY REPORT OF THE FREEDOM LEAGUE AND THE FREEDOM RESEARCH FOUNDATION, MAY 1988.

in August 1986, Weyrich, William Kling, and other conservatives conducted a seminar on "political technology" in Santiago for nearly one hundred activists.[65]

A July 1988 forum in Santiago, Chile, sponsored by Weyrich's International Policy Forum, was one of three trips William Kling made to Chile in 1988. The forum was funded by the National Endowment for Democracy (NED) through the Republican Party. The NED was established to give U.S. government funds publicly to groups conducting activities identical to those which were historically funded covertly by the Central Intelligence Agency. A similar forum in Argentina was also NED-funded through the U.S. Chamber of Commerce. Free Congress materials were distributed there in Spanish.[66]

William Kling also meets regularly with other experts on Latin America in Washington including former U.S. National Security Council staffers Constantine Menges, Jose Sorzano, and Roger Fontaine. Sam Dickens of the American Security Council, as well as the Ambassadors from Guatemala and Chile are also part of the hard-right foreign policy network run by Kling.[67]

The *Freedom Fighter* is co-published by the Freedom League from Weyrich's offices through the effort of Charles Moser, treasurer of the FCF board of directors. (*See left*)[68] The monthly newsletter, which reports on right-wing paramilitary forces worldwide, is co-published along with Dr. Jack Wheeler's Freedom Research Foundation. Wheeler has been a speaker at many right-wing events, including meetings of the World Anti-Communist League. At the 1984 meeting, Wheeler praised RENAMO and introduced its representative to the audience. The representative made the false claim that South Africa had cut its links to RENAMO.[69]

Freedom Fighter reported and supported the activities of RENAMO, which the State Department and others estimate has massacred about 100,000 Mozambicans. U.S. Deputy Assistant Secretary for Africa Roy Stacy said RENAMO had conducted "one of the most brutal holocausts against ordinary human beings since World War II." A military organization without a distinct political program, RENAMO's function was to destabilize the Mozambican government. It was supported by elements in the U.S. and Europe and received support and direction from South Africa.[70]

UNITA was also supported by *Freedom Fighter* and WACL. Another South African-allied operation, UNITA's function was to destabilize the Angolan government, enhancing Pretoria's power in southern Africa. Weyrich signed a Conservative Caucus ad calling for support to UNITA. Additionally *Freedom Fighter* supported the Nicaraguan Contras, Islamic fundamentalists in Afghanistan, and similar groups in Cambodia, Laos, and Vietnam.[71]

The FCF says that they distribute the *Freedom Fighter* newsletter to members of Congress, the executive branch, media, and public policy analysts. *Freedom Fighter* is edited by Warren Carroll, a former Central Intelligence Agency employee who founded Christendom College, a small, right-wing Catholic school in Virginia. Former Deputy Central Intelligence Agency director Vernon Walters sits on its board and FCF staffer William Marshner teaches theology there. The college receives annual grants from the Coors family foundation. [72]

FREE CONGRESS FOUNDATION DIRECTORS ALSO IN THE COUNCIL FOR NATIONAL POLICY

The FCF has substantial interactions with New Right groups through its coalition activities, staff liaisons, and its board of directors. This is strikingly evident in FCF's ties to the Council for National Policy, a secretive meeting and planning group for the New Right described later in this report. FCF's Connie Marshner and eleven of seventeen of the Free Congress directors are also CNP members. Paul Weyrich is the CNP's Secretary-Treasurer. [73]

Other Free Congress Foundation directors in the Council for National Policy include:

■ **John D. Beckett**, Chairman of the Board of Directors of Intercessors for America (IFA) and, with Connie Marshner, a member of the Coalition on Revival (COR) steering committee. Intercessors' newsletters indicate that the group is involved with shepherding discipleship cult leaders, as does Beckett's COR leadership position. The newsletters also express concerns about Freemasonry. IFA directs supporters to pray for Star Wars and "godly" governments and candidates. IFA'ers are also encouraged to "Pray for the Pretoria government, especially President Botha and President Reagan. . ." as well as for the Intercessors branch in South Africa. Beckett is also on the CNP's Board of Governors. IFA has been supported by the Coors Foundation. [74]

■ **Robert Billings**, an early CNP member, is on the advisory board of Intercessors for America, as are Paul Weyrich, Rev. Pat Robertson, Ed McAteer, and Rev. Tim LaHaye. Billings is vice-chairman of the Free Congress board of directors. The co-founder of Moral Majority has described himself as "the liaison between Congress and the Christian community." (*More on Billings later*) [75]

■ **Howard Long**, owner and CEO of Coronet Foods Inc., recently joined the CNP.

■ **Marion Magruder**, President of McDonald's Restaurants in Arizona, has given CNP $20,400 since 1986.[76]

■ **U.S. Senator William Armstrong** is associated with many New Right, especially Christian Right, causes. He is on the advisory board of Intercessors for America.

■ **James Hill, Jr.**, a Houston-based real estate developer, is active nationally and in Australia. He is a member of CNP's Board of Governors.

■ **Robert Krieble**, a retired Connecticut businessman, is secretary of FCF's board of directors and with CNP's Board of Governors, as well as a number of other rightist elements, such as the Rockford Institute, a Coors-funded organization whose board also includes Edwin Feulner. He is also a member of CNP's thirteen-member executive committee.[77]

■ **Richard DeVos** is president of Amway and is also a member of CNP's executive committee and Board of Governors. DeVos was CNP's president from 1986–88. He was an early backer of behind-the-scenes efforts in the mid-1970's to stimulate the Religious Right to make the U.S. "a Christian Republic." Avon Products, in a letter to DeVos rebuffing Amway's attempted takeover of Avon, called Amway "morally bankrupt and criminally corrupt." Avon said, "Your company is an admitted criminal. . . .Your corporate culture is marked by zealotry." DeVos also serves on the Chairman's Council of the Conservative Caucus, a group allied with right-wing and white supremacist elements in southern Africa. Conservative Caucus spends most of its efforts aiding these elements.[78]

■ **Thomas A. Roe** is one of the fifty-five members of CNP's Board of Governors, and a board member of International Policy Forum, another group headed by Weyrich. Roe is active in a number of far-right groups and is chairman of the Roe Foundation.[79]

OTHER FREE CONGRESS FOUNDATION DIRECTORS

Other Free Congress Foundation directors include Faith Ryan Whittlesey, Kathleen Teague Rothschild, and Charles Moser, who is treasurer of the FCF board:[80]

■ **Faith Ryan Whittlesey** headed the White House Office of Public Liaison in Reagan's second term. In that position, she was deeply involved in organizing domestic support for the Contras. Whittlesey established the White House Outreach Working Group on Central America, which according to *The New York Times* disseminated the Reagan Administration's view that "Nicaragua is a Communist beachhead threatening the hemisphere and. . .the American public is not being fully informed of the danger." Whittlesey has said that the American media unfairly ignored human rights violations by the Sandinistas. [81]

■ **Kathleen Teague Rothschild** for many years was chair of the FCF's board of directors. During that period, she was also on the board of the U.S. Council for World Freedom, which is the U.S. branch of the World Anti-Communist League (WACL), home for many fascists and neo-Nazis. The U.S. branch brought these elements to the U.S. for WACL's annual meetings in 1984 and 1985. Included was a delegate who served five years in prison for attempting to assassinate Charles DeGaulle, persons who led Nazi SS units or collaborationist puppet governments during World War II, and architects of mass murder in Latin America. Those meetings served to build support for the FDN Contras as well as UNITA and RENAMO, both allies of South Africa. The U.S. branch, headed by Major General John Singlaub, also has had racists, anti-Semites and at least one member of a Nazi collaborationist organization on its board.[82]

■ **Charles Moser** is active in several Weyrich groups, including the *Freedom Fighter* newsletter and Coalitions for America. In the name of the latter group, he wrote proposals for forming six committees that would support right-wing paramilitary forces in six countries, including UNITA in Angola. The Free Angola Committee was organized in 1982 with a five-member board and operated out of the Committee for a Free Afghanistan office. The Committee for a Free Afghanistan was started with money from the Heritage Foundation and the Free Congress Foundation and supports the extreme Islamic fundamentalists in Afghanistan. Moser was treasurer of the Committee for a Free Afghanistan. He also proposed committees for Vietnam, Cambodia, El Salvador, and Nicaragua. The latter committees never became active. The proposed Nicaragua committee was dominated by persons who had received support from Moon's Unification network and by the leader of a Moon-related group.[83]

Dr. Jack Wheeler, a supporter of the brutal RENAMO forces, was a speaker at the Council for National Policy's February 1989 meeting.

UPPER LEFT & RIGHT:
COUNCIL FOR NATIONAL POLICY, MEETING PROGRAM, FEBRUARY 1989, ORLANDO, FLORIDA.

Senator William Armstrong (R-CO) serves on the FCF Board of Directors and the Board of Reference of Intercessors for America. Others on the Intercessors board include Paul Weyrich, Pat Robertson, Ed McAteer, Tim LaHaye, and Robert Billings. This type of overlapping of directorates is common in the rightist networks funded by the Coors family.

Convicted Nazi collaborator Laszlo Pasztor works closely with Paul Weyrich through Weyrich's Coalitions for America, a group housed at the Free Congress Foundation building complex in Washington, D.C.

COALITIONS FOR AMERICA DESCRIPTIVE BROCHURE.

INTERCESSORS FOR AMERICA

Gary Bergel
President

BOARD OF DIRECTORS
John D. Beckett *
Chairman
Em Baxter
Warren Black
Jay Fesperman *
John Heard *
Jimmy Owens
Derek Prince
John Talcott
Larry Tomczak
* Executive Committee

BOARD OF REFERENCE
Dr. Ben Armstrong
Senator William Armstrong
Dr. Robert J. Billings
Dr. Bill Bright
Rev. Gerald Derstine
Dr. Richard C. Halverson
Rev. Jack W. Hayford
Dr. E.V. Hill
Rt. Rev. John Howe
Mrs. Dee Jepsen
Dr. Tim LaHaye
Mr. Ralph Martin
Mr. E.E. (Ed) McAteer
Mr. M.G. (Pat) Robertson
Mrs. Edith Schaeffer
Mr. Paul Weyrich
Dr. B.J. Willhite

February 16, 1990

Dear IFA Undergirder:

    Grace, peace and strength to you in Christ Jesus!

    Thank you for the prayers you have been offering for us here at Intercessors for America. We are in a busy time of year but are sensing a hedge of protection and a release into strategic areas that cut across denominational, cultural and

March 15–18, 1990 an IFA team is ministering in Vancouver, British Columbia. Pastor Jim McNally, my oldest son, Ian and I are going to strengthen and encourage the believers in Vancouver and Canada who have taken a stand in Christ against the first international homosexual olympic games scheduled for August 11–14, 1990. Pray for our protection, for wisdom and for anointing. Bind spirits of anti-Christ, perversion and sodomy.

Intercessors for America (IFA) is a rigidly homophobic right-wing Christian fundamentalist group. John D. Beckett, President of Intercessors for America, sits on the board of directors of the Free Congress Foundation, which is run by Paul Weyrich and funded by the Coors family. INTERCESSORS FOR AMERICA, FEBRUARY 16, 1990.

FASCIST AND ANTI-SEMITIC NETWORKS

FCF DIRECTOR MOSER AND
UKRAINIAN NAZI COLLABORATIONIST NETWORKS

F CF director Charles Moser is on the editorial advisory board of the
Ukrainian Quarterly, published by the Ukrainian Congress Committee
of America (UCCA). The UCCA is an umbrella group of Ukrainian
groups in the U.S. and is dominated by the Organization of Ukrainian
Nationalists (OUN), a secret cadre organization sponsored by Nazi Germany until the end of World War II. It still makes pronouncements that
reflect national socialist ideology. Among the groups in UCCA is a "veterans group of the First Ukrainian Division," which until 1945 was known
as the 14th Waffen SS Division under the control of the German Nazi Party.
Other UCCA components are known for their anti-Semitic propaganda.[84]

Moser's *Ukrainian Quarterly* continues to defend the history of
Ukrainian collaboration with Nazism and has led the fight to oppose U.S.
investigations into Nazi war criminals in the United States. Its attempts to
obscure and revise World War II history would be obvious to anyone who
regularly receives the *Quarterly*, which is presumably the case with editorial
advisers.[85]

In 1985, the Weyrich-sponsored Coalitions for America, housed at the
FCF offices, issued a statement to Congress calling for measures that would
have greatly hindered the Justice Department investigations of suspected
Nazi war criminals. At the time, Weyrich was president of the group,
Connie Marshner was vice-president, and Moser was treasurer.[86]

PAUL WEYRICH'S SPONSORSHIP
OF A NAZI COLLABORATOR

When the press reported the presence of emigré Nazis in the Bush campaign
in the fall of 1988, Laszlo Pasztor, one of the rightists forced out of the
campaign, was reported as working part-time at Weyrich's Free Congress
Foundation.[87]

Pasztor is a convicted Nazi collaborator who served a prison term for his
role in World War II as a functionary in a Hungarian pro-Nazi party, the
Arrow Cross, and his service in a wartime Hungarian diplomatic delegation
to Berlin after the Nazis installed the avidly pro-Nazi Arrow Cross as the
government of Hungary.[88]

Pasztor denies he was ever a pro-Nazi or anti-Semite. Pasztor claims that
during late 1944 he was in Berlin "on a secret mission to trick the Germans."
Pasztor also claims to have a document from the Hungarian government
stating he was never condemned as a war criminal. Pasztor's critics, however,
never called him a war criminal; they have called him a collaborator with

the Nazis who participated in the fascist anti-Semitic Arrow Cross party during the war years. The letter produced by Pasztor scarcely resolves those charges. Holocaust historian Randolph L. Braham dismisses Pasztor's claims of innocence as "lies."[89]

In 1969, Richard Nixon gave Pasztor permission to organize a permanent ethnic arm of the Republican Party. Pasztor brought in Central and Eastern Europeans who were Nazi collaborators, alleged war criminals, and officials of Nazi puppet governments from the wartime era. Pasztor also brought these groups into the American Security Council's Coalition for Peace through Strength. (See ASC elsewhere in this report)[90]

Pasztor says that the FCF provides him with office space for his work for the Weyrich-sponsored Coalitions for America, and that he regularly provides written reports of his activities to Weyrich, who is president of FCF as well as national chairman of Coalitions for America. The Coalitions for America brochure uses a photograph of Pasztor to illustrate the work of the Liberation Support Alliance. Pasztor's official title is National President of the Liberation Support Alliance which "seeks to liberate peoples in Central and Eastern European nations." The Liberation Support Alliance is a constituent part of the Resistance Support Alliance which seeks to aid anti-communist forces in Asia, Africa, and Central America. The Resistance Support Alliance is in turn a constituent group of the Weyrich-sponsored Coalitions for America, a group housed at the FCF building in Washington, D.C. and run by Eric Licht, a long-time Weyrich associate and former Free Congress Foundation vice-president for development.[91]

In early 1989, according to Pasztor, a Bush Administration White House staffer asked him for a list of names of fellow Hungarian-Americans to be invited to a special private briefing on the political and economic situation in Hungary. The briefing was conducted April 3, 1989 at the Old Executive Office Building next to the White House. Members of the National Security Council and State Department were said to be in attendance. According to an Administration source, Pasztor was on the original invitation list but was asked not to attend after other federal agencies raised questions regarding Pasztor's background in the Arrow Cross.[92]

Pasztor says he has helped "obtain assistance for the anti-communist democratic opposition behind the Iron Curtain from the National Endowment for Democracy," a tax-funded institution which funds political operations which enhance U.S. foreign policy objectives. NED has made grants for projects in Hungary. Pasztor says he has provided translations and acted as an intermediary for Hungarian and Czechoslovakian groups and has helped them apply for funds from the NED's National Republican and National Democratic Institutes for International Affairs, as well as the

(Left to Right) **Paul Weyrich, Vice President-elect Dan Quayle, and Free Congress Foundation executive vice president Jim Constantino discuss policy recommendations presented to the incoming Bush Administration.** *ABOVE & BELOW:* FREE CONGRESS FOUNDATION, ANNUAL REPORT, 1988

Free Congress Foundation Board of Directors. Back Row *(left to right):* **Marion Magruder, Jr., Dr. Charles Moser, Ph.D., Jeffrey H. Coors, Paul M. Weyrich, Howard W. Long, John D. Beckett, Dr. Robert H. Krieble. Front Row** *(left to right):* **Michelle Laxalt, Richard DeVos, Dr. Robert J. Billings, Kathleen Teague Rothschild, Thomas A. Roe, James Martin Hill, Jr., Ambassador Faith Ryan Whittlesey.** *Not Pictured:* **Senator William L. Armstrong, Congressman Ralph M. Hall, Stephen Walsh.**

German Marshall Fund. According to Pasztor, several of the grant applications he handled were funded.[93]

Pasztor also spoke at a forum co-sponsored by the Heritage Foundation and the Anti-Bolshevik Bloc of Nations (ABN). The ABN was founded in 1943 in alliance with Hitler's war on the eastern front. It was composed of political and paramilitary units that had aided Hitler's occupation of the region, including forces from the Ukraine, the Baltic region, Hungary, Byelorussia, and Bulgaria. Some ABN leaders were implicated in war crimes. The leadership of the ABN did not change dramatically after World War II, nor did the group's expressions of national socialist ideology. The ABN became the Eastern European branch of the World Anti-Communist League (WACL). According to an ABN publication, Pasztor spoke as a representative of the "Hungarian organization." The same issue of *ABN Correspondence* has a full-page obituary for an official of a Nazi puppet government during World War II.[94] Following the political upheavals in Eastern Europe, FCF leader Weyrich visited Hungary on behalf of the Free Congress Foundation to train political organizers.[95]

In 1989, a resurgence of anti-Semitism was noted in some small Eastern European political parties, including the Democratic Forum (MDF) in

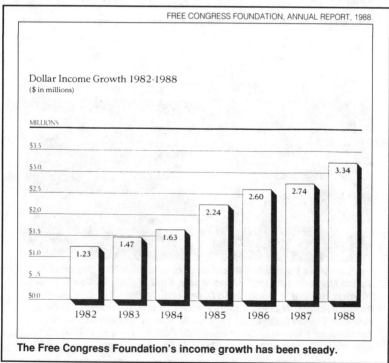

FREE CONGRESS FOUNDATION, ANNUAL REPORT, 1988.

Dollar Income Growth 1982-1988
($ in millions)

MILLIONS

	1982	1983	1984	1985	1986	1987	1988
	1.23	1.47	1.63	2.24	2.60	2.74	3.34

The Free Congress Foundation's income growth has been steady.

Hungary. One *Newsweek* article noted anti-Semitic comments by MDF activist Istvan Csurka. Pasztor says he met with MDF leaders in a 1989 trip to Hungary.[96]

COORS MONEY POURS RIGHT

The current chairman of the board of the Free Congress Foundation is Jeffrey Coors, continuing a long history of family support for Weyrich's organizational activities. In 1988, the Coors Foundation, controlled by Jeffrey, Peter, Joe, and William Coors, gave Free Congress $150,000 to support its operations. From 1977–88, the Coors family has given an additional $127,000 to the Free Congress Political Action Committee (formerly CSFC), enhancing Weyrich's Capitol Hill influence. The Federal Election Commission says that FCF-PAC has one of the most voluminous filings on record, indicating extensive fundraising, campaign support, and disbursements. No single donor source, however, matches the Coors family contributions.[97]

The FCF-PAC has also supported Christian extremists, giving their two largest donations in 1986 to the shepherded Mark Siljander and to Joseph Morecraft, a follower of R.J. Rushdoony (*see the CNP section*) and ally of the late John Birch Society leader Larry McDonald. Morecraft is also on the Coalition on Revival steering committee.[98]

It is not known what additional support individual members of the Coors family or the Coors corporation have given to the FCF network.

THE COUNCIL
FOR NATIONAL POLICY

SHAPING A NEW RIGHTWARD
VISION FOR AMERICA

One of several key rightist groups that has long been supported by the Coors family is the Council for National Policy (CNP). The Council is a secretive group of the foremost right-wing activists and funders in the United States. Morton Blackwell of the CNP has said, "The policy [of CNP] is that we don't discuss who attends the meetings or what is said." Its membership, meetings, and projects are all secret, even though the group enjoys tax exempt status. It focuses on foreign policy issues.[99]

The Council actually has two related organizations, the Council for National Policy, the tax exempt 501(c)3 membership group, and CNP, Inc., a 501(c)4 element set up in 1987. The latter group will allow the parent Council to lobby and engage in legislative matters without jeopardizing its tax exempt status. Since the Council (hereafter referred to as CNP) intends to maintain a very low visibility, it is likely that members lobbying at the behest of CNP or CNP, Inc. will use the names of other groups with which they are affiliated.[100]

Individuals pay $2,000 per year to be a member of the CNP. For $5,000, one can become a member of the Council's Board of Governors, which elects the executive committee of CNP. That executive committee then selects the officers on an annual basis. Members of CNP are encouraged to give part of their membership fee to CNP, Inc.[101]

The CNP was founded in 1981 when Tim LaHaye, a leader of Moral

Majority, proposed the idea to wealthy Texan T. Cullen Davis.[102] Davis contacted billionaire Nelson Bunker Hunt, and from that point on they began recruiting members. By 1984, the Council had four hundred members.[103]

Joe and Holly Coors were early members of the CNP. Their names appear on a 1984 confidential list of members. Also on the list is Lt. Colonel Oliver North, retired generals John Singlaub and Gordon Sumner, and other Contra network supporters, such as former ambassador Lewis Tambs, Louis (Woody) Jenkins, and Lynn (L. Francis) Bouchey. Sumner, Tambs, Bouchey, and CNP member Frank Aker are also leaders of the Council for Inter-American Security (CIS), a group with ties to the Rev. Sun Myung Moon's far-flung political network. (See "Coors versus Pluralism" later in this report)[104]

The first president of CNP, from 1981–82, was founder Tim LaHaye. He was a militant anti-humanist who once criticized Michelangelo and Renaissance art for its nude figures, which he claimed were "the forerunner of the modern humanist's demand for pornography. . ."

LaHaye and others brought together representatives from the Religious Right, the White House, elected officeholders, the political right, and right-wing businessmen. They conceived of themselves as a rightist alternative to the establishment Council on Foreign Relations in New York City. The CNP's first executive director, Louisiana State Representative Woody Jenkins, told members, "I predict that one day before the end of this century, the Council will be so influential that no President, regardless of party or philosophy, will be able to ignore us or our concerns or shut us out of the highest levels of government."[105]

Council members who are willing to discuss the CNP at all describe its main function as a forum for bringing activists and wealthy funders together to plan projects of mutual interest. One member said that the 1985 campaign to pressure Reagan to fire then Secretary of State George Schultz (for not being sufficiently supportive of South Africa) began at a CNP meeting.[106]

Although a former staffer told a Baton Rouge newspaper that Oliver North never directly asked for money, North did make the Contras' needs known to CNP members. He addressed their quarterly meetings at least three times in the mid-1980's, once distributing pictures of a Nicaraguan airfield. Ellen Garwood, who was active in WACL meetings and donated funds to the Contras, told the Congressional Iran-Contra Committees that she first met Oliver North at a CNP meeting.[107]

Tom Ellis succeeded LaHaye in 1982 as president of the CNP. Ellis is a top political operative of Jesse Helms, running various political organizations that make up the Helms empire. Ellis was a director of one of the groups which supports the Helms network—the Pioneer Fund, a foundation which finances efforts to prove that African-Americans are genetically inferior to whites. Ellis has said, "The eventual goal of this movement [racial integration] is racial intermarriage and the disappearance of the Negro race by fusing into the white." While Ellis has since disavowed his segregationist position, his associates in the Helms organizational network are still tied to the Pioneer Fund board and receive Pioneer funds.[108]

Recipients of Pioneer grants have included William Shockley, Arthur Jensen, and Roger Pearson. Pearson has written that "inferior races" should be "exterminated." All three, and others, were funded during Ellis' directorship on the Pioneer board. Yet Ellis served on the CNP's thirteen-member executive committee with Holly Coors, Paul Weyrich, and Heritage Foundation president Edwin Feulner until June 1989. Oliver North and Reed Larson of the anti-union National Right to Work Committee recently joined the executive committee.[109]

After Ellis' one-year term as president of CNP in 1982–83, he was succeeded by Nelson Bunker Hunt, Pat Robertson, and Richard DeVos of the Amway Corporation. Some of the other board members of the Council for National Policy also have colorful pasts.[110]

BOARD MEMBERS OF
THE COUNCIL FOR NATIONAL POLICY

■ **Richard Shoff** is owner of Lincoln Log Homes in North Carolina. A former Ku Klux Klan leader in Indiana, Shoff is a financial supporter of High Frontier, a Star Wars group allied with a tiny occult group headed by Elizabeth Clare Prophet called the Church Universal and Triumphant. Shoff also supports the Conservative Caucus, a group which cheerleads for the apartheid regime in South Africa. Shoff was recently implicated in a questionable fundraising scheme shut down by the Attorney General of Illinois. Funds collected under the name "Children with AIDS Foundation" were slated to support a homophobic right-wing religious activist, Rev. H. Edward Rowe, and a group of private investors, but the funds were allegedly paid to investors and fundraisers, with no funds spent on any actual projects.[111]

■ **Jay Parker** is a former registered agent for a territory of South Africa, paid for by the South African regime.[112]

■ **John McGoff** was exposed as a partner in a secret South African government attempt to buy newspapers in the U.S. as covert propaganda outlets. McGoff serves on the editorial advisory board of the *Washington Times* which frequently supports the South African apartheid government in news and editorial columns. The *Washington Times,* part of Moon's Unification network, received an award from the Council for National Policy in 1984.[113] According to reporter Murray Waas, South Africa bought into a secret partnership arrangement with the *Washington Times* in 1982.[114]

■ **Don McAlvany,** a frequent traveler to South Africa, has held meetings with South African military and police groups to organize pressure to get the South African government to disavow the Alvor accords that ended warfare against Angola and SWAPO on April 1, 1989. While in South Africa, McAlvany suggested that someone might want to kill Archbishop Desmond Tutu but immediately retracted the statement. He is a contributing editor to the John Birch Society's weekly, *New American.* [115]

■ **James McClellan** is a Helms associate active in repealing civil rights legislation. He is also an associate of racialist Roger Pearson.[116]

■ **Ben Blackburn** is a former member of Congress noted for opposing civil rights legislation. He is also a past board chairman of the Heritage Foundation.[117]

■ **David Noebel** is now with Summit Ministries and was a former Associate Evangelist of Billy James Hargis' Christian Crusade, which built itself in part during the 1950's through racist appeals, primarily in the South. Noebel wrote two books in the 1960's: *Communism, Hypnotism and the Beatles* and *Rhythm, Riots and Revolution.* The latter book attempted to prove that folk music was a communist plot.[118]

■ **William D'Onofrio** is a member of the National Association for Neighborhood Schools (NANS), a group formed to stop busing to achieve racial integration which attracted some unsavory supporters and leaders such as Ralph Scott. Scott has ties to the racialist Pioneer Fund and has endorsed racist writings. Former NANS president James Venema has said, "Ralph Scott is credited with being the father of NANS." (Ralph Scott is also a past vice-president of DANK, the German-American National Congress, a group Lucy Dawidowicz, author of the definitive *The War Against the Jews 1933–1945,* characterizes as pro-Nazi.) D'Onofrio is also the Maryland coordinator for the Conservative Caucus.[119]

■ **Robert Weiner** is head of Maranatha, a "shepherding discipleship" religious cult. He directs members to do political work for rightist causes and candidates.[120]

■ **R.J. Rushdoony** is ideological leader of the "Christian Reconstruction" movement. He advocates that Christian fundamentalists take "dominion" over the U.S., abolish democracy, and institute the death penalty for children who disobey their parents. According to *Christianity Today*, Rushdoony also believes, "True to the letter of Old Testament law, homosexuals . . . adulterers, blasphemers, astrologers, and others will be executed." He believes there is no need for the U.S. Constitution and calls democracy a "heresy." He was a featured speaker at a 1983 Free Congress Foundation Conference on Criminal Justice Reform. FCF's conference literature described Rushdoony as a "prominent Christian writer."[121]

■ **Gary North**, another Christian Reconstructionist, has written the following statement concerning abortion, "How long do we expect God to withhold His wrath, if by crushing the humanists who promote mass abortion. . . . He might spare the lives of literally millions of innocents?"[122] His Institute for Christian Economics advocates a system of slavery out of which Christians could work their way after a set period of time. Since the CNP is deeply involved in foreign policy issues, it is worth noting that North believes:

> The so-called underdeveloped societies are underdeveloped because they are socialist, demonist and cursed. The Bible tells us that the citizens of the Third World ought to feel guilty, to fall on their knees and repent from their Godless, rebellious socialist ways. They should feel guilty because they are guilty, both individually and corporately.[123]

■ **Robert Grant** is chairman of Christian Voice and American Freedom Coalition. The former group is tied to "shepherding discipleship" while the latter is a political front for Moon's Unification network and has threatened to form a hard-right political party.[124]

■ **Rev. Jerry Falwell** for many years has been leader of the Moral Majority and still is a major force in the televised evangelical movement.

■ **Ron Godwin**, formerly second in command at Moral Majority, now is an executive for Moon's Unification network's *Washington Times* newspaper.[125]

■ **Reed Larson** is head of the National Right to Work Committee. Henry Walther, also formerly of this anti-union group, is a CNP member as well. Larson's group receives support from the Coors Company.[126]

■ **Morton Blackwell**, who also has received Coors support for a number of years, is president of International Policy Forum. IPF trains right-wing conservatives around the world in New Right political techniques. A longtime associate of Paul Weyrich, who chairs IPF, Blackwell was one of the New Right activists attempting to take over the American Independent Party (*see the Free Congress Foundation section*) in 1976. To his credit, he was

COUNCIL FOR NATIONAL POLICY
Officers
1983-1984

Mr. Nelson Bunker Hunt, President

Mr. Bob J. Perry, Vice President

Mr. Paul Weyrich, Secretary-Treasurer

Rep. Louis (Woody) Jenkins, Executive Director

Mr. Thomas F. (Tom) Ellis,
Immediate Past President

EXECUTIVE COMMITTEE
Members

Mr. Joseph Coors (Thru May 1984)

Mr. Rich DeVos (Thru May 1985)

Mr. Thomas F. Ellis (Thru May 1986)

Mr. Nelson Bunker Hunt (Thru May 1986)

Mr. James F. Justiss (Thru May 1985)

Dr. Tim LaHaye (Thru May 1986)

Mr. Sam Moore (Thru May 1985)

Mr. Howard Phillips (Thru May 1985)

Dr. Pat Robertson (Thru May 1984)

Mr. Richard Viguerie (Thru May 1984)

Mr. Paul Weyrich (Thru May 1984)

Presidents of the
Council for National Policy

Dr. Tim LaHaye, 1981-1982

Mr. Thomas F. Ellis, 1982-1983

Mr. Nelson Bunker Hunt, 1983-1984

Thomas Jefferson Award
COUNCIL FOR NATIONAL POLICY
1981-1983

1981	Honorable David Stockman, Director, Office of Management and Budget
1982	Ambassador Jeane Kirkpatrick, U.S. Ambassador to the United Nations
1983	Senator Jesse Helms (R-North Carolina)

Special Achievement Awards
COUNCIL FOR NATIONAL POLICY
1982-1984

1982	Family Law Mrs. Phyllis Schlafly, President, Eagle Forum
1982	International Law Congressmen Jack Fields (R-Texas)
1982	Broadcasting Dr. Pat Robertson, President Christian Broadcasting Network
1983	National Defense Dr. John Lehman, Secretary of the Navy
1983	Magazine Publishing Dr. Beurt SerVaas, President SerVaas, Inc.
1983	Health Education and Research Dr. Cory SerVaas, Publisher, *Saturday Evening Post*
1984	International Broadcasting Mr. Frank Shakespeare, Chairman, Board of Radio Free Europe/Radio Liberty
1984	Free Enterprise Mr. Sam Moore, Chairman Thomas Nelson Publishers

The leaders of the Council for National Policy listed in this 1984 meeting program reflected a range of ideologies from conservative to reactionary and hard-right.

COUNCIL FOR NATIONAL POLICY, MEETING PROGRAM, MAY 1984, WILLIAMSBURG, VIRGINIA.

THE Five Minute Report

May 26, 1989

FOR AND ABOUT THE MEMBERS OF THE COUNCIL FOR NATIONAL POLICY

On behalf of The Conservative Caucus Foundation, CNP member, Howard Phillips has been attending board meetings of major American corporations involved in arrangements which may transfer hard currency resources and/or technology to the Soviet Union. He has attended stockholder meetings of RJR Nabisco, Chevron Corporation, Texaco, and Eastman Kodak. At the Chevron Corporation meeting, Chevron chairman Ken Derr told Howard, on the record, that Chevron would withdraw from Communist Angola if requested to do so by President Bush.

EXECUTIVE COMMITTEE MEMBERS
1989-90

Holly Coors, Rich DeVos, Ed Feulner, Bob Krieble, Reed Larson, Connie Marshner, Oliver North, Howard Phillips, Paul Pressler, Ed Prince, Mike Valerio, Richard Viguerie and Paul Weyrich.

EXECUTIVE COMMITTEE OFFICERS
1989-90

Paul Pressler......President
Bob Krieble...Vice President
Paul Weyrich......Secretary-
                  Treasurer

The Council for National Policy networks rightists through secret meetings and this restricted circulation newsletter with chatty reports on members' activities.

A Training School For Communists

The John Birch Society launched a major campaign against the civil rights movement, especially its leadership. Attacked in this *American Opinion* postcard distributed by the JBS is the Rev. Martin King, Jr. *(right, labeled 1).* AMERICAN OPINION POSTCARD.

the foremost voice opposing the GOP's electoral collaboration with neo-Nazi cult leader Lyndon LaRouche in 1976. More recently, however, his Leadership Institute has been providing political campaign training to members of Maranatha, the shepherding cult.[127]

■ **Don Wildmon**, whose campaign against the movie *The Last Temptation of Christ* was charged with using anti-Semitic propaganda, is a member of the steering committee of COR. Wildmon has claimed that Universal Studios is "a company dominated by non-Christians." Wildmon also regularly threatens television networks with boycotts for "indecent" content in their programs.[128]

■ **Phyllis Schlafly** is a leading anti-feminist who first came to national attention as an ardent anti-communist. She claimed the Republican Party was controlled by an elaborate conspiracy of bankers and financiers who were assisting a global communist conquest. In *A Choice Not an Echo*, Schlafly says that the "New York kingmakers . . . some of whom profess to be Republicans. . .favor aiding and abetting Red Russia."[129] Schlafly defends as a hero the late Cardinal Mindszenty of Hungary, a noted anti-communist who has been called a pro-feudalist, anti-Semitic collaborationist who did little to stop the German Nazi massacre of Hungarian Jews.[130]

Other figures representing anti-feminist politics, Radical Right religious activities, and pro-South Africa and pro-Contra activists are members and supporters of CNP. Of special note among unsavory characters in the CNP is Robert K. Brown, publisher of *Soldier of Fortune* (SOF) mercenary magazine. *Soldier of Fortune* has regularly praised pro-Nazi individuals and groups, and promotes the sale of Nazi regalia. SOF started in 1975 in sympathy with the racist regime of Rhodesia. In recent years, SOF staff has trained Salvadoran officials in urban warfare. SOF has also bragged that *Soldier of Fortune* T-shirts are part of the Nicaraguan Contras' uniform.[131]

ORIGINS OF THE CNP

The origins of the CNP are not found in mainstream conservatism or the traditional Republican Party but in the nativist and reactionary circles of the Radical Right, including the John Birch Society. The view on the Radical Right that an organization such as CNP was needed stemmed from their perception that the Council on Foreign Relations (CFR)—closely identified with the Rockefeller family—was selling out American interests in the pursuit of an imagined left-wing foreign policy agenda. This conspiratorial critique was begun in earnest about thirty years ago by the John

Birch Society. In 1972, the Society promoted *None Dare Call it Conspiracy*, a book that identified the CFR as procommunist.[132]

The CFR is more accurately described as a highly influential group of bankers, businessmen, academics, generals, and media representatives that has dominated U.S. foreign policymaking for decades. It has promoted a complicated Cold War strategy against the USSR during that period that employed psychological warfare, covert operations, diplomatic gambits, and pressures from economic warfare and military encirclement. These measures were designed to be used in a carrot-and-stick fashion to cause the eventual diminution and dissolution of the USSR and the Warsaw Pact.

The Radical Right, led by the John Birch Society (JBS), preferred an even more confrontational approach with the USSR and the imposition of what amounted to fascist-style dictatorships on underdeveloped countries that showed signs of independence from U.S. influence or domination. The John Birch Society has probably been the foremost source of U.S. rightist propaganda in the last thirty years. It advocated repression at home and abroad for political expressions that challenged U.S. hegemony. It created confrontational politics along a whole range of local, national, and foreign policy issues.

In the 1960's, the Society organized against the civil rights movement and widely circulated material portraying Rev. Martin Luther King, Jr., and the civil rights movement as controlled by communists. Another JBS campaign fought sex education. The JBS, long run in a dictatorial manner, has warned repeatedly of the dangers of democracy. A *New American* essay entitled "This is a Republic Not a Democracy!" claims, "The central problem with the rise of unlimited democracy and universal suffrage is that the Whig relationship between property ownership and voting has been severed." Books written several years after the 1958 founding of the JBS describe it as a racist and anti-Semitic organization, although in recent years JBS has attempted to distance itself from those earlier views.[133]

Birch Society membership peaked at slightly over 100,000 in the mid-1960's, following the Society's successful organizing effort inside the ill-fated 1964 Goldwater presidential campaign. Goldwater expressed discomfort with both the Birch and other Radical Right support for his candidacy, and, later, he criticized some of the more zealous beliefs of the New Right, but his candidacy served as a benchmark for both of those movements. The Goldwater campaign inadvertently also provided the organizational and financial basis for the New Right when fundraiser Richard Viguerie obtained copies of the Goldwater campaign's list of contributors and began single-issue, direct mail fundraising projects which raised both money and consciousness among conservatives and rightists. As the New Right grew in influence, the Birch Society, and many of its Old Right organizational allies, lost strength. Yet the Society still maintained significant influence on the right throughout the 1960's and early 1970's. Wealthy businessmen such as Joe Coors gave money to the JBS, and his company bought ads in their publications. When Coors was a regent at the University of Colorado he distributed JBS literature to other regents.[134]

In the 1970's, Birch organizers created single-issue front groups that helped build the base of the Radical Right. The Birch front groups fought against busing, sex education, taxes, gun control, police reform, civil rights, and women's rights (especially the ERA and reproductive rights). The JBS groups sought to keep the U.S. in Vietnam and get it out of the United Nations. Before and after the 1980 campaign, the Birch Society and other Radical Right constituencies were wooed by the New Right. As author Alan Crawford observes:

> [T]he Birchers seem to have wormed their way back in along the frontier of the New Right. The New Right leaders seem to welcome them. The New Rightists may indeed feel more comfortable with the primitive Birchers than they do with *National Review* types, whom they regard as effete Easterners; indeed, when this author worked at *Conservative Digest* in 1975, the editors kept back copies of both Birch periodicals, *American Opinion* and the *Review of the News*, in the office, but not back copies of the more moderate conservative weekly *Human Events*.[135]

The New Right played an important role in the 1980 election of President Ronald Reagan and sought to consolidate its gains by expanding its institutional presence in Washington, D.C. New Right leaders created the CNP in part to develop alternative foreign policy initiatives to oppose those offered by the Council on Foreign Relations. The CNP organizes support for confrontational policies long sought by Radical Rightists and ultra-conservative hawks. Support for the "Reagan Doctrine" of so-called "low-intensity" warfare was one outgrowth of this effort. The CNP also addresses domestic social and cultural issues. In many foreign policy matters and domestic issues, the CNP frequently reflects a slick, updated repackaging of Birch Society philosophy.

The Birch influence on the political goals of the CNP is significant. The JBS was with CNP from the beginning. Nelson Bunker Hunt, mentioned earlier as a prime mover in CNP's founding, was on the Birch Society's national council. By 1984, John Birch Society Chairman A. Clifford Barker and Executive Council Member William Cies were CNP members. Other JBS leaders also joined the Council. Five board members of Western Goals, essentially a JBS intelligence-gathering operation (and later used to funnel aid to the Contras), joined the CNP as well.[136]

While it should not be argued that the CNP is a creation of the Birchers, its very existence is a testament to the success of the JBS goal of creating a rightist counterpoint to established power. The CNP has become a player in mainstream political life in the United States. Ambassadors, prominent public figures such as Milton Friedman, members of Congress and the executive branch have addressed CNP meetings. James Quayle, father of the Vice President, and other key political supporters of Dan Quayle have been nominated for CNP membership, as the Council seeks to expand its influence.[137]

The CNP is selectively expanding its membership as well. One of the more recent members is Jeffrey Coors, who joined Holly and Joe Coors on the Council in 1987. He has contributed $16,200 since joining the Council, while Holly has contributed $30,750 over the last six years. Jeffrey is a member of the Board of Governors of the Council, as is Robert Walker, the retired director of national affairs for Coors in Washington. Walker contributed $20,000 during a four-year period while he worked for Coors.[138]

Other indicators of Coors family commitment to the Council come from the Coors Foundation, which gave $20,000 to the CNP from 1985 to 1988. In a recent Council event, at least six members of the Coors family participated, including Jeffrey and his wife.[139]

THE COORS FAMILY EXTENDED POLITICAL NETWORK

There are dozens of political and Religious Right groups funded by Coors. Since a substantial amount of Coors money comes from family members' personal accounts, the extent of Coors family involvement cannot be fully known and a full listing of such groups cannot be compiled here. A brief description of several key groups follows.

NATIONAL STRATEGY INFORMATION CENTER (NSIC)

The National Strategy Information Center (NSIC) was founded in 1962 by Frank Barnett. It has been a longtime recipient of Coors money, and Joe Coors has been on the Center's advisory board for a number of years.[140]

The NSIC conducts programs and publishes materials promoting what they call "low-intensity warfare" or "low-intensity conflict." Advocates of such warfare, including NSIC, see low-intensity conflict as shifting from locale to locale. In practice it is an endless, ongoing, permanent form of paramilitary action against governments and political movements that assert independence from U.S. domination. The fomenting of civil wars and assassination are standard methods of such control, and NSIC is one of the foremost groups promoting such carnage. As early as 1961, Frank Barnett, who would later become NSIC director, advocated "political warfare" abroad that included promoting "diverse forms of coercion and violence including strikes and riots, economic sanctions, subsidies for guerrilla or proxy warfare and, when necessary, kidnapping or assassination of enemy elites."[141]

In 1983, the NSIC co-sponsored a "symposium" on "low-intensity" war with a Pentagon component in a continuing effort to build support for such policies. (It should be noted that it is only low-intensity warfare from a U.S. government perspective, where nuclear war scenarios are considered high-intensity. Nevertheless, it can be a major and brutal civil war in a Third World country or a pacification program, as in Guatemala, where tens of thousands of people have been killed.)[142]

The NSIC has been closely identified with U.S. intelligence, especially the Central Intelligence Agency. The NSIC-Pentagon symposium engaged many former CIA station chiefs and covert operations personnel, as well as military personnel.[143]

The Washington office of NSIC runs a project called Consortium for the Study of Intelligence which produced a nine-volume series on intelligence issues such as covert action and subversion that critics have called at best authoritarian and at worst a potential blueprint for a police state.[144]

The Consortium is directed by NSIC Washington director Roy Godson, a consultant since 1982 to the President's Foreign Intelligence Advisory Board, which oversees covert operations. He also has been a consultant to the National Security Council. The Consortium engages many current and retired intelligence agency employees, including Robert Gates, who was also deputy director of the Central Intelligence Agency while working on the NSIC project. Gates was later denied the Central Intelligence Agency director's job because of his role in the Iran-Contra affair but in 1991 was again proposed for the position. He was deputy director of the National Security Council. Gates addressed a Free Congress Foundation meeting in 1989 after receiving his NSC post. Robert Walker, director of national affairs for the Coors Corporation from 1982 to 1988, is also a consortium member.[145]

AMERICAN SECURITY COUNCIL FOUNDATION (ASCF)

Another organization that has enjoyed Coors support is the American Security Council Foundation (ASCF), the fundraising and education arm of the American Security Council (ASC). It is also the "educational secretariat" for the American Security Council's Coalition for Peace

Through Strength. Joe Coors served on the ASCF board through the 1980's.[146]

The ASC was formed in 1955 as a worker blacklisting operation, screening potential employees for what management defined as unacceptable views. ASC once claimed to have the "largest private collection on revolutionary activities in America," described in *Newsweek* as "a card file of six million names, including peaceniks, draft card burners, and pseudo-intellectuals." ASC became a nexus between military contractors and retired generals, lobbying for higher military budgets and more weapons programs. Throughout its history it has networked persons with racist and fascist politics.[147]

In 1978, the ASC and ASCF invented the Coalition for Peace Through Strength to enhance its lobbying strength and to network conservatives around hard-line military issues. Brought into the Coalition were groups with fascist, white supremacist, racialist or anti-Semitic backgrounds. Some had links to Nazi Germany, having aided Hitler's war effort.

Roger Pearson's Council on American Affairs was brought into the Coalition, and Pearson was made a board member of ASC's American Foreign Policy Institute. He also became an editor of the *Journal of International Relations*, published by the Center for International Security Studies, an ASC-affiliated group.[148]

The ASCF was active in the New Right election victories of Ronald Reagan and right-wing senators in 1980. Activities included the production of films such as *Attack on the Americas*, concerning Central America, and a 1984 sequel. A campaign film was also produced in 1984 to support weapons programs and politicians who supported those programs. A speakers bureau and direct-mail were also apparently used for electoral ends by the tax exempt group.

Other ASCF board members with Joe Coors included the late Karl Bendetsen, architect of the detention program of Japanese-Americans during World War II, and Lady Malcolm Douglas-Hamilton. Douglas-Hamilton is related to a British family that supported Hitler's war aims. When she and her husband came to the U.S., he helped establish a branch of the Military and Hospitaller Order of Saint Lazarus of Jerusalem, an obscure racist-led network based in Scotland and tied to Jesse Helms.[149]

The ASCF also created a "Strategy Board" in the early 1980's that included a number of persons with covert operations backgrounds, including Major General John Singlaub; the late Edwin Black, who was implicated in drug and gunrunning operations linked to the Nugan-Hand bank; Ray Cline, a former Central Intelligence Agency covert operations director long active with the World Anti-Communist League; and Ed Feulner, the president of the Heritage Foundation.[150]

COORS AND THE RELIGIOUS RIGHT

Although the Coors family has been a well-known supporter of groups such as the Heritage Foundation and the Free Congress Foundation, less well-known are the family ties to the Religious Right. The family has contributed substantially to Falwell's Moral Majority, for instance.

The Religious Roundtable is a network of fifty-six religious and political right-wing leaders which was formed a decade ago to help coordinate activities. Jerry Falwell is on the Council of Fifty-Six of the Religious Roundtable; Pat Robertson resigned from the Roundtable board in 1986. The Roundtable describes ASC president John Fisher and Joe Coors as good friends of the organization.[151]

The Coors family has supported right-wing religious fundamentalist broadcaster Pat Robertson. Holly Coors is a board member of the Christian Broadcast Network's Regent University—formerly CBN University—a component of the Robertson network. In 1988, the Adolph Coors Foundation gave $50,000 to Regent University, adding to the several hundred thousand dollars from previous years. In 1986, Joe Coors announced that he was leaning toward Pat Robertson for the 1988 presidential race; he mentioned his great respect for Robertson. A former administrative assistant to Coors in the 1970's, Carolyn Sundseth, later headed Americans for Robertson. Sundseth worked in the Reagan White House after leaving Coors where she was Joe's administrative assistant. While heading the Robertson group, she also joined the steering committee of the Coalition on Revival, a group described earlier that is heavily influenced by shepherding, discipleship, and Christian Reconstructionism.[152]

It is worth noting that CBN is not just interested in the propagation of right-wing religious ideology at home but has been deeply involved with pro-Contra propaganda and direct aid to Contra forces in Central America. It has also been supportive of RENAMO in Mozambique.[153]

In 1988, the Coors Foundation also donated $15,000 to the Institute on Religion and Democracy (IRD), a group that mobilizes religious sentiment for ultra-conservative and reactionary political goals. IRD's anti-Sandinista themes in the early to middle 1980's have been supplemented with other Cold War subjects in recent years. IRD attacks mainstream religious leaders and denominations for not supporting right-wing foreign policy goals. Some IRD principals, such as Penn Kemble, were also tied to secret Contra support projects.[154]

AMERICAN SECURITY COUNCIL
FOUNDATION

John M. Fisher
President

October 9, 1982

Dear Friend:

The KGB has privately taken a lot of the credit for nuclear freeze victories such as the 3 to 1 landslide vote for the nuclear freeze in the state of Wisconsin in mid-September.

KGB leaders tell the Kremlin that their orchestration of the nuclear freeze movement through the World Peace Council is their greatest disinformation success.

Major General Richard Larkin, USA (Ret.), former Deputy Director of the Defense Intelligence Agency, tells me that the KGB is spending, "$300,000,000 to put on a year's activities in the United States. This is apart from their salaries and their travel-expenses."

If this sounds strong, read John Barron's article in the October Reader's Digest detailing KGB manipulation of the freeze movement.

Even this enormous cost is just the start because most of the organizations in the United States which are helping fund the freeze campaign are not Communist.

They are the same anti-defense activist groups which have long agitated for sharp cuts in our defense budget --- major groups like the American Friends Service Committee, National Council of Churches, and the World Council of Churches.

The freeze-niks have raised tens of millions of dollars in the United States. For example, in just one Los Angeles rally they raised $750,000.

On the other hand, the Los Angeles Times couldn't find any anti-freeze group which had been able to raise money against the nuclear freeze resolution on the California ballot in November.

American Security Council Foundation material, often jingoistic, routinely proposes aggressive military solutions for a wide range of foreign policy problems.

AMERICAN SECURITY COUNCIL FOUNDATION FUNDRAISING LETTER.

The Conservative Caucus (TCC), frequently the major U.S. cheerleader for supporting more rigid policies by the apartheid government of South Africa, also sought to block the prosecution of Lt. Col. Oliver North. North inscribed a note on this photo with TCC's Howard Phillips *(right)*, **used in a TCC fundraising letter.**

THE CONSERVATIVE CAUCUS

Another New Right group with long-standing ties to (and financial support from) Coors, is The Conservative Caucus (TCC), headed by Howard Phillips. The group is not truly conservative but is among the most radical of reactionary groups in the U.S. It claims 600,000 members, but that figure does not refer to dues-paying members, which is a much smaller number. Inflated membership figures and a long list of names on the letterhead does not obscure the fact that the Conservative Caucus can only maintain a staff of five and an additional five on Phillips' tax exempt Conservative Caucus Foundation.[155]

The long list of TCC "Executive Advisory Board" members includes Joe and Holly Coors. Joe Coors has been a longtime associate of the Conservative Caucus. In early 1977 he was a member of the Citizens Cabinet Organizing Committee, a TCC project which established a shadow cabinet in February 1977 to counter the incoming Carter Administration. Also on the Committee was Coors aide John McCarty, Heritage president Frank Walton, Paul Weyrich, Richard Viguerie, William Rusher, Larry McDonald, and Howard Phillips. The Committee was formed only months after Phillips, Rusher, Viguerie, and Weyrich had attempted to lead the Klan-infested American Independent Party. The alternative cabinet proposed by Coors and his allies had a number of leading John Birch Society figures and supporters among its twelve members, and Phillips continues to work closely with the John Birch Society and its allies.[156]

The Conservative Caucus (TCC) has been active on a range of issues since it was founded by Phillips in 1974. In the last several years, however, TCC has worked on southern Africa issues in alliance with the South African government. After the South African government signed accords which gave SWAPO the possibility of gaining power in Namibia and which obligated the apartheid regime to cut its support to Jonas Savimbi's UNITA operation in Angola, the Conservative Caucus criticized the accords. TCC has since attacked the ruling Nationalist Party of South Africa as selling out to the Soviet Union. Phillips has recently quoted favorably the head of South Africa's openly white-supremacist Conservative Party. TCC board member Don McAlvany works with military and police officials in South Africa who are perceived as supporting a harder line than the Nationalist Party. Phillips and McAlvany have organized numerous two-week trips to South Africa for Americans to meet top political party and business leaders as well as military intelligence officials who are not allowed into the United States. These trips are advertised in John Birch Society publications.[157]

So committed is Phillips to the UNITA operation that he traveled to Jamba in Angola to meet with UNITA's leader, Jonas Savimbi. He and

Michael Johns of the Heritage Foundation tried to persuade Savimbi to come to the U.S. in the spring of 1989 to lobby for continued U.S. funding of UNITA. (Johns was the editor of Jerry Falwell's now-defunct *Liberty Report* while also an editor at the Heritage Foundation's *Policy Review*.) Phillips lobbies the Bush Administration and Capitol Hill for UNITA. TCC attempts to counter critics of UNITA's human rights abuses and has run newspaper ads on UNITA's behalf. Phillips appears to advise Savimbi regularly on how to lobby Congress and appears to follow Savimbi's wishes regarding strategy. Although it has widely lobbied in support of UNITA, the Conservative Caucus has not chosen to register as a foreign agent for UNITA.[158]

Another Conservative Caucus board member and funder is Richard Shoff, a North Carolina businessman whose questionable business practices have brought him the attention of local newspapers, trade associations, and the Better Business Bureau. Shoff has also been involved in a number of lawsuits while running sales operations in Indiana and selling log homes from his company, Lincoln Log Homes, in North Carolina. Shoff also came to the attention of Klan watchers when he lived in Indianapolis. In the early 1970's, he was the Grand Kilgrapp (state secretary) of the Indiana Ku Klux Klan. Indianapolis police told a reporter that KKK cross burnings were held on Shoff's property during Klan rallies which were hosted by Shoff. According to the head of the Indiana KKK, Shoff was also a generous funder of Klan activities. Shoff claims he left the Ku Klux Klan in 1973.[159]

Shoff is also on the board of Coalition for Freedom, a Jesse Helms group that receives funding from the Pioneer Fund which funds racialist research.[160] Shoff is one of a number of TCC leaders who are also members of the Council for National Policy. Other Conservative Caucus supporters and leaders who are also members or leaders of the Council for National Policy include Amway leader Richard DeVos, Louis Jenkins, and Robert H. Krieble, John D. Beckett, and Joe and Holly Coors.[161]

THE COORS FAMILY
VERSUS PLURALISM

THE COORS FAMILY AND WOMEN

The Coors family tradition reflects a belief in conservative family and sex roles. In this tradition, women belong in the home and men belong in the boardroom. In the division of corporate responsibilities between the children of brothers William and Joe Coors, this gender-based, anti-woman approach to family role and status is dramatically evident. Joe Coors' five sons assumed leadership positions within the company; William's daughters received no corporate appointments. A Coors son can expect gifts of stock, and an education at Exeter followed by engineering studies at Cornell University and the Colorado School of Mines. A Coors daughter is expected to marry wisely and may receive a home as a present.

Sons are political leaders. Peter Coors hinted in 1988 that he may want to run for the United States Senate. Coors daughters and wives maintain a low public profile although Joe Coors' wife Holly did have several ceremonial titles while her husband was in Reagan's "Kitchen Cabinet." One reporter noted that when Holly married Joe Coors, she "entered a world where it went without question that the men ruled, the women obeyed. And for the next forty-eight years, she did just that."[162]

The Coors corporation itself has reflected the family bias against women. When the Equal Employment Opportunity Commission brought suit against Coors in 1975, only seven percent of the employees were women. There were not even restroom facilities for women production workers until 1973.[163]

Joe Coors was actively anti-feminist and a financial supporter of Phyllis Schlafly's organization opposed to the Equal Rights Amendment, STOP-ERA. Schlafly's anti-ERA campaign released a brochure, "The ERA-Gay-AIDS Connection," which argued that the ERA would "give the homosexuals a weapon to impose their anti-family lifestyle on our society" and would prevent society from protecting "itself against a class of people who have a high rate of various contagious diseases (some fatal)." Another Schlafly brochure warned that the ERA would require state-funded elective abortions and quoted approvingly from an anti-abortion activist's analysis of the Equal Rights Amendment, "The ERA mentality is the source of today's social evils—hostility toward women, preborn babies, men, family, church, state, and God."[164]

Although William Coors has said he supports the ERA, Coors family funding and support continues to be directed to groups and individuals that espouse an anti-feminist point of view, including the Free Congress Foundation, the Heritage Foundation, the Mountain States Legal Foundation, Pat Robertson, Tim LaHaye, Jerry Falwell, and the Moral Majority. These groups advance a "pro-family" agenda, which opposes abortion, federally-supported day-care, divorce, gay and lesbian rights, drug abuse, pornography, and secular humanism. The pro-family movement supports traditional values, which include prayer in the schools, chastity until marriage, the ideal American family as envisioned by the conservative mind (men work and women raise the children), and educational reform, including tuition tax credits, voucher programs, home schooling, and parental control of education.

Tim LaHaye, husband of Beverly LaHaye (who heads Concerned Women for America, a prominent pro-family organization), is the founder and first president of the Coors-supported Council for National Policy. Tim LaHaye has claimed that day-care is a "secular humanist plot to steal the hearts and minds of millions of little children." LaHaye, author of *The ACLU: One of the Most Harmful Organizations in America* and *The Unhappy Gays*, also believes that pornography, and the ACLU lawyers who defend pornographers, are the real culprits in cases of child abuse. More than any other single entity, pornography, he says, has "destroyed lives, marriages, and families, brought grief to children and caused a catastrophic increase in child molestation." In an August 1989 fundraising letter, LaHaye said, "You see, most people believe mothers should be encouraged to stay home and raise their children rather than letting day care centers raise them. But not our liberal leaders. . . . Our liberal leaders don't believe a pro-family woman can be fulfilled by staying home and raising her children. So they're pushing the radical feminist agenda."[165]

The Coors family are longtime, loyal supporters of Pat Robertson, contributing money and time to advance Robertson's ministry. Like Jerry Falwell and LaHaye, Robertson is a minister who advocates a Bible-based, pro-family agenda. Robertson, a faith healer, also claims to have controlled the course of a hurricane by directing it away from his headquarters. Like LaHaye, he believes that only Christians or Jews should hold political office in the United States. Robertson has spoken in harsh terms of those who reject his moral view, telling one reporter:

> If you wanted to get America destroyed, if you were a malevolent, evil force and you said, "How can I turn God against America? What can I do to get God mad at the people of America to cause this great land to vomit out the people?" Well, I'd pick five things. I'd begin to have incest, I'd begin to commit adultery, wherever possible, all over the country, and sexuality. I'd begin to have them offering up and killing their babies. I'd get them having homosexual relations, and then I'd have them having sex with animals.[166]

But despite his fervent embrace of a strict, conservative Christian morality, Robertson repeatedly misstated his wedding date to obscure the fact that his child was born ten weeks after his marriage. When Robertson's wife, Dede, was six months (or eight months, depending on the report) pregnant, almost destitute, and responsible for the care of their infant child, Robertson left home for a month-long religious retreat to Canada. His wife tried to stop him, saying, "I'm a nurse. I recognize schizoid tendencies when I see them and I think you're sick." Robertson left anyway and Dede wrote him a frantic letter, saying, "Please come back. I need you desperately." Robertson responded, "I can't leave. God will take care of you."[167]

Jerry Falwell and his organization Moral Majority have received financial support from the Coors family. Falwell has been deeply involved in the anti-ERA movement. In a fundraising letter, Falwell said, "With all my heart I want to bury the Equal Rights Amendment once and for all in a deep dark grave. The liberals keep resurrecting this anti-family legislation that, if passed, could damage the American family and all the moral values we hold so dear here in America." One reporter quoted Falwell's description of women in the feminist movement, "Leaders of the feminist movement are 'blasphemers,' and the feminist movement is 'a satanic attack on the home' led by 'uncaring women who have failed.' "[168]

Jerry Falwell, Pat Robertson, and Tim LaHaye have worked together on pro-family issues over the years. They believe that men and women have different natures and roles, assigned by God and beyond question. All three men condemn feminism and believe that government should penalize nontraditional sex roles. Since they see the legitimacy of U.S. criminal codes as

COORS' CORPORATE IMAGE

When it comes to developing innovative and supportive programs for women, we at Coors have made a commitment to go the extra mile.

In the past three years, we've distributed more than 720,000 breast self-examination cards across the world to help fight the battle against breast cancer.

We've also become a significant sponsor of women's athletics, including pro rodeo, collegiate softball and national amateur softball tournaments. And to help inspire the next generation of women athletes, we have underwritten a Parent's Guide to Girls Sports.

Our "Volunteers Under 30" program is encouraging young women across the country to get involved in the cause of their choice and to discover how good it feels to give.

To keep you informed of what we're doing, we have created an annual publication that celebrates women everywhere. To receive your free copy of "Hurrah!" simply write to us at Coors Community Relations, NH420, Golden, CO 80401. You see, our work has only just begun.

© 1989 Coors Brewing Company, Golden, Colorado, 80401. Brewer of Fine Quality Beers Since 1873.

Our Women's Work Is Never Done.

The Coors Brewing Company purchases image advertising in women's and feminist publications. This 1989 ad encourages "young women across the country to get involved in the cause of their choice and to discover how good it feels to give."

©1989, COORS BREWING COMPANY, GOLDEN, COLORADO, 80401. THE COORS LOGOTYPE IS A REGISTERED TRADEMARK.

COORS' FAMILY FUNDING

THE JOURNAL OF
FAMILY
AND
CULTU

SPRING 1988

School-based Clinics
& Moral Civil War
Donna Steichen

Is Tax Simplification
Good for Families?
Robert M. Willan

Divinity, Philosophy & Dur
A Primer for Parents
Charles Helms

Principles, Problems & P
Mark Rodgers

VOLUME III, NU

SCHOOL-BASED CLINICS
AND MORAL CIVIL WAR

by Donna Steichen

A MERICANS everywhere are talking about adolescent sexuality. Conflict about whether and how government should address the issue, philosophical differences about morality, the role of schools, children's rights, family autonomy, and effective social policy are part of an open "battle for the morals of the children." [1]

Growing numbers of Americans see "value-free" sex education, government-funded birth control, clandestine provision of contraceptives and abortions as leading inevitably to out-of-wedlock pregnancies. Since large scale federally-sponsored birth control began in 1970, the incidence of sexually transmitted disease among teenagers has soared, too, often with permanent consequences in sterility. Recent reports that AIDS has been diagnosed in some high school students stirs more intense alarm: is "safe sex" advice the best society can offer to protect children from a disease that is sordid, painful, and fatal?

Educational reformers, including Secretary of Education William Bennett, and people worried about a national ethical crisis, point to casual teenage sexual activity, pregnancy, abortion and venereal disease as symptoms of social decay. They demand that public schools emphasize character education.

At the same time, a high-visibility public relations drive by members of the birth control establishment, warning about a "national epidemic" of "children having children" at the rate of "more than a million teenage pregnancies every year," has converted its campaign slogans into conventional wisdom in the minds of many others. Irreversible changes in sexual mores make adolescent sexual activity inevitable, they say, proposing to avert the worst consequences with

The Coors family funds a variety of anti-feminist groups and is a major funder of the Free Congress Foundation which publishes organizing materials for those fighting abortion rights and seeking to limit dissemination of information about birth control.
©1988, FREE CONGRESS RESEARCH AND EDUCATION FOUNDATION.

derived from Judeo-Christian morality, sins such as adultery, homosexuality, and bestiality should also be criminal offenses. All three have been highly visible activists within the Coors-funded pro-family network.

Coors' advocacy of gender inequality has had enduring impact through Coors-funded political organizations, such as the Mountain States Legal Foundation (MSLF), the Free Congress Foundation, and the Heritage Foundation. In 1979, the Mountain States Legal Foundation, with Joe Coors as a funder and director and James Watt as president, filed a successful federal suit to block the extension of the ERA ratification process. Maxwell A. Miller, the Foundation's senior lawyer, claimed "[the lawsuit] was our idea and our work product from the beginning to end." Miller is also an associate of the white supremacist Roger Pearson.[169]

Connie Marshner was a founding editor of the *Family Protection Report*, published by the Free Congress Foundation's Center for Child and Family Policy; she is a frequent contributor to the *Report's* successor, *Family, Law and Democracy Report*. Marshner is involved with the Coalition on Revival (COR) and the Word of God, described earlier in this report. She and Michael Schwartz, also of the FCF, are on the Advisory Council of the Couple to Couple League International, which opposes all contraception other than chastity. The Couple to Couple League claims, "A return to chastity and the extermination of the contraceptive mentality is absolutely necessary for both the Church and our society as a whole."

In 1988, the Free Congress Foundation and the Heritage Foundation jointly released *Issues '88: A Platform for America*, a three-volume study of the ideal political platform "for a stronger and healthier America based on sound conservative principles." This study, by two influential Coors-financed groups, provides perhaps the most comprehensive view of the "pro-family" vision for the United States.[170]

The *Issues '88* program, which is recommended as a model Republican Party platform, would criminalize abortion, either through a constitutional amendment or through the reversal of *Roe v. Wade*. The program would also restrict the availability of divorce, calling divorce "the major contributing factor to the so-called feminization of poverty." Although Heritage and FCF say they want to limit government regulation, in fact, they propose an enormous intervention in the personal lives of all adults: "Divorce laws should also require specific and serious grounds because the *state's interest* is in keeping marriages intact. This state interest is rooted not only in practical concerns arising out of the social cost of divorce but also in the recognition that families are the basic unit of society, and the state, therefore, has a right and duty to *foster marriage* and marital stability." [author's emphasis][171]

Heritage and FCF argue for the appointment of a guardian to represent children in divorce proceedings, but this guardian's only task is to prevent the divorce since "keeping the marriage together should be considered, as a matter of law, the primary interest of the children." The only section in which child abuse is discussed is titled, "Restore common sense to child abuse reporting"; it calls for "better protection of the rights of accused parents." Although rape is briefly mentioned in the section on crime, *Issues '88* presents no strategy to combat the rape and battery of women by men. [172]

The Heritage/FCF program opposes minimum wage laws, rent control, comparable worth, and "high" welfare payment levels which bring recipients to or above the poverty level (these "encourage welfare dependency"). It supports mandatory, full-time workfare programs, home education, school prayer, and the routine testing of schoolchildren for HIV antibodies, and for illegal drug use. [173]

The *Issues '88* response to teenage pregnancy is a requirement that sex education "encourage young girls to 'just say no' to premarital sex." The program calls for parental consent for abortion, sex education, and distribution of contraceptives. Heritage and Free Congress Foundation would abolish school-based health clinics, which dispense contraceptives and discuss abortion as an option when counseling pregnant students, because they "promote the values of Planned Parenthood." *Issues '88* notes that a parental consent requirement would limit abortions because parents would need to grant their daughter "permission to take the life of their grandchild" before she could have an abortion. [174]

Issues '88 strongly supports what is called the "right" of women to work in the home on cottage industry piecework. The program claims the ban on work in the home hurts the elderly and the handicapped and is "particularly harmful to mothers." The proposal to "end barriers to work in the home" notes that "big business could create thirteen million new jobs at home." This work is discussed as a boon to the family; the work would "strengthen the family by allowing parents to nurture and care for their own children." In reality, home work is a boon to big business which would reap the benefits of non-union (and virtually unorganizable) workers, of not having to invest in production sites, and of low, piecework pay scales. The phrasing of this proposal reflects its business bias—*Issues '88* refers repeatedly not to the rights of those who work at home but to "the right of employers to hire employees based at home." The FCF/Heritage proposal does not address the fact that jobs currently based at corporate worksites would be lost to homework, causing dislocation and suffering to many wage earners and their families. They not only advocate repealing laws and regulations banning homework but also seek to gut minimum wage laws. Little concern for the real economic advancement of the family can be found here. [175]

To push their agenda in Congress, Heritage and Free Congress Foundation advocate an aggressive approach to discredit liberals and malign the motives of those who do not accept the conservative vision. Liberals are described as "extremists," "anti- family," "minority factions," and "guardians of mediocrity." They are repeatedly defined as "interest groups," "special interest groups," "powerful special interests," and "an entrenched network of special interests." Liberals have "far-left agendas," they are allied with "extremist groups," they "rob families to pay bureaucrats," use "misleading tactics," and support proposals which are "neither compassionate nor effective."[176]

When Heritage president Ed Feulner and FCF's Paul Weyrich jointly signed the introduction to the *Issues '88* program in 1988, Jeffrey Coors (until recently CEO of the Coors corporate empire) was FCF chair. Heritage received $100,000 from the Coors Foundation in 1988 and Free Congress received $150,000.

THE COORS FAMILY AND GAY RIGHTS

> **" Joe Coors' sons are also in harmony on at least one other point: Homosexuals are an abomination in the eyes of God. "**

Los Angeles Times
1988

The Coors family maintains strongly held, fundamentalist religious beliefs. In a profile of the Coors family in 1988, the *Los Angeles Times* noted that "All five of Joe Coors' sons, inspired by their mother, Holly, 67, are self-described born again Christian Fundamentalists. . . . The whole family is awaiting Armageddon, which Joe Jr. believes will occur around the year 2000." Also, according to the article, the Coors family "haggles over such diverse matters from George Bush's choice of running mate to whether AIDS is, in fact, God's pre-Armageddon punishment of homosexuals."[177]

They can work with ease with the social issues-oriented New Rightists such as Paul Weyrich. Since Jeffrey Coors became chair of Weyrich's Free Congress Foundation (FCF), the Coors Foundation's annual contribution to FCF has increased fifty percent to $150,000. And FCF is actively mobilizing public fear of the gay and lesbian communities. FCF's "Senior Contributing Scholar" Father Enrique Rueda wrote in a 1987 book, *Gays, AIDS and You,* "once you understand the agenda of the homosexual movement, you will probably perceive it as a terrible threat—to ourselves, our children, our communities, our country."[178]

The thesis of the Rueda book is that "this movement is using the AIDS crisis to pursue its political agenda. This in turn, threatens not only our values but our lives." Rueda, who is himself using the AIDS crisis to pursue a political agenda, asserts that "homosexuality . . . is a psycho-sexual dysfunction" that is "gravely sinful by the very nature of reality." Nevertheless, he claims to have discovered that "the homosexual movement . . . has a coherent ideology." It should be combated with "a well-organized campaign within the schools, professional and religious bodies, economic institutions, and the media . . . should the pro-family forces prevail, homosexual acts would come to be viewed as a manifestation of sinfulness, an illness or a potential and/or actual source of crime."[179]

Enrique Rueda is not the only person who plans to make being a gay man or lesbian a crime. In 1988, Paul Weyrich of the Free Congress Foundation and Edwin Feulner of the Heritage Foundation jointly released what they called an ideal platform for the 1988 elections, with several hundred planks. One plank, "Halt AIDS and Sexually Transmitted Diseases," said that fighting AIDS would require "such policy actions as: reintroducing and enforcing anti-sodomy laws." The same plank also argues that all public school children in middle or high schools should be regularly tested for HIV antibodies, as should public employees, and the entire populations of hospitals, drug abuse treatment programs, and prisons. The government was warned against "official pandering to small socially destructive special interests." [180]

Many other Coors-supported groups express similar views. Morality in Media is another group that has received Coors funding for many years. Morality in Media of Massachusetts organized a Boston forum in 1985 at which one speaker advocated the use of an old leper colony in Boston Harbor for the quarantine of people with AIDS. Co-sponsors along with Morality in Media included the speaker, Vernon Mark, director of neurosurgery at Boston City Hospital, and Helen Valerio, who along with her husband Michael Valerio, owns the Papa Gino's restaurant chain. The Valerios are longtime, right-wing political activists, and Papa Gino's is a major funder of the FCF. At the time of the conference, Joe Coors was then a member of Morality in Media's board of directors. In 1988, the Coors Foundation gave $15,000 to Morality in Media.[181]

When Jeffrey Coors attends Council for National Policy (CNP) meetings, he may secretly meet (as is the nature of CNP events) with other homophobic people such as Jerry Falwell, who has a long history of anti-gay activism. He also might chat with R.J. Rushdoony, who advocates executing homosexuals. He certainly encounters dozens of others who believe, as he does, that homosexuals are an abomination. The views of the CNP membership seem to be compatible with his personal views on a range of issues,

COORS' CORPORATE IMAGE

To improve its reputation and expand its sales, the Coors Corporation purchases image-enhancing advertising in gay and lesbian publications around the country.

©1989, COORS BREWING COMPANY, GOLDEN COLORADO 80401. THE COORS LOGOTYPE IS A REGISTERED TRADEMARK.

COORS' FAMILY FUNDING

This Man Wants His "Freedom" So Bad He's Ready To Let America Die For It.

He fights like a warrior possessed, on the front lines of the Gay Rights movement. Our civilization stands in the path of his fulfillment as a freely promiscuous homosexual. And he's willing to sacrifice our freedom, our families, and even our lives to get his way.

GAYS, AIDS AND YOU explains the Gay Rights movement in America, its power, and how it uses the AIDS epidemic to gain political ground. Factual, hard-hitting, GAYS, AIDS AND YOU is a must for the 20th century American who intends to help preserve our traditional values and standards of morality.

And our civilization.

For your copy, fill out the coupon and send check for $4.95 (plus $1. shipping) to

Free Congress Foundation
721 Second Street N.E.
Washington, D.C. 20002

ORDER FORM
Please send me ___ copies of GAYS, AIDS AND YOU.
Enclosed is $_____ ☐ Check ☐ Visa ☐ Master Card
Credit Card Number_____ Exp. Date_____
Signature_____
Name:_____
Address: _____
City: _____ State: _____ Zip:_____

The Coors family funded Free Congress Foundation is one of the nation's largest distributors of virulently homophobic literature.

FREE CONGRESS FOUNDATION, ORDER FORM FOR *GAYS, AIDS AND YOU*, BY RUEDA AND SCHWARTZ.

including homophobia. When Jeffrey castigated his father (Joe Coors) for running off to California with a young mistress in 1988, he called him "a sinner, along with homosexuals, gluttons, blasphemers, murderers, liars" according to a characterization of Jeffrey's remarks by the *Los Angeles Times*.[182]

The Coors company has used polygraph testing in screening prospective employees or investigating employees in their plants. The Coors polygraph operator who screened prospective employees or investigated current employees is reported to have routinely asked questions about one's sex life, such as whether one was married, single, or divorced, had single or multiple sex partners, frequency of sexual activity, etc. Questions on one's political views were also asked. This kind of intrusive polygraph testing was one of the issues that motivated the 1977 Coors strike. Coors representatives would later deny that Coors used the polygraph for such purposes, although a number of affidavits, sworn testimony before the Senate, and press reports indicate that Coors did indeed use the polygraph to impose its narrow political views and quest for sexual conformity upon the workers. In its associations with right-wing political groups, Coors tries to impose those same views on the entire American public.[183]

THE COORS FAMILY AND AFRICAN-AMERICANS

The Coors family has had a history of racist practices and support for groups that maintain racist ideas or promote programs that would adversely affect the African-American community. In recent years, the Coors Company has obscured this fact by signing pacts with several Black organizations that have resulted in some Coors-controlled funds going into Black-owned banks and African-American community projects.

The Coors family practiced restrictive hiring policies in their company to such an extent that the federal Equal Employment Opportunity Commission charged in 1975 that the Coors Company had intentionally engaged in discriminatory practices over the previous ten years. The EEOC filed suit in the U.S. District Court in Denver on September 9, 1975. Coors settled out of court on April 22, 1977, just ten days after the AFL-CIO boycott began.[184]

The Colorado Civil Rights Commission had also found the Coors Company guilty of racial discrimination in the 1969 firing of a Black employee. When hired in 1962, the employee, Booker T. Mays, was only the second Black employee at Coors. He told the Civil Rights Commission that during the 1960's he was the victim of racial harassment at Coors. He was reinstated with back pay to his job.[185]

During the 1964 Civil Rights Act debate in Congress, William Coors called the virtually all-white Coors work force together to encourage them to oppose the passage of the bill. He told them that sixty white employees would be replaced with Blacks if the bill passed. The meeting took place while employees were on paid company time.[186]

The best known incident reflecting William Coors' racism was a 1984 speech he gave to a minority business group in Denver. He told the group that if they thought it was "unfair" that their "ancestors were dragged here in chains against their will. . . . I would urge those of you who feel that way to go back to where your ancestors come from, and you will find out that probably the greatest favor that anybody ever did you [sic], was to drag your ancestors over here in chains, and I mean it."[187]

Later in the speech, Coors elaborated on what he saw wrong in Africa:

> . . . the government of these nations that have gotten the right of self-determination, that's where the operation of the government, the operation of the businesses, has switched primarily from white to Black—it's not that the dedication among the Blacks is any less. As a matter of fact, it is greater. There's tremendous motivation there, because they perceive themselves as being free people to succeed. They lack the intellectual capacity to succeed, and it is just taking them down the tubes. You take a country like Rhodesia, where the economy was absolutely booming under, you might say, white management. Now, Black management is in Zimbabwe, and the economy is a disaster, in spite of the fact that there is probably ten times the motivation on the part of the citizens of that country to make it succeed. Lack of intellectual capacity—that has got to be there.

After he suggested that 250 years of slavery was a gift of history to African-Americans, and trotted out vicious old images of Black mental incapacities, several African-American organizations joined the ongoing boycott of Coors. One joint advertisement by African-American elected officials, the Urban League, a ministerial alliance and others criticized Coors' comments and "Coors' current associations with the apartheid government of South Africa." [188]

Support for apartheid was and is manifest by the various groups that Coors started and in which the family is active. A report by the *Christian Science Monitor* noted that "a shadowy ethnic German organization" in Namibia (Namibia was under German control until the turn of the century and has been under South African control since then) was seeking financial support from the Heritage Foundation. The Heritage money, in conjunction with efforts by South African military intelligence, was to be used to

The Coors Corporation has purchased image advertising in Black-owned magazines and publications aimed at African-Americans. The company distributes press releases stressing its outreach to the Black business community and has signed contracts with a number of minority firms.

©1989, COORS BREWING COMPANY, GOLDEN COLORADO 80401. THE COORS LOGOTYPE IS A REGISTERED TRADEMARK.

EARLY CIVILISATIONS OF THE NORDIC PEOPLES

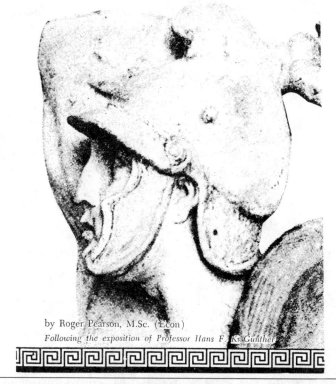

by Roger Pearson, M.Sc. (Econ)
Following the exposition of Professor Hans F. K. Günther

The Coors Family has funded and worked with an interlocking network of groups which have harbored racists, racial eugenicists, a former Ku Klux Klan leader, even a convicted Nazi collaborator. The Coors family funded Heritage Foundation once placed Dr. Roger Pearson, the author of this ode to white supremacy, on an editorial advisory board, and the Coors Foundation bought subscriptions to other Pearson publications for Colorado libraries. ©1965, THE NOONTIDE PRESS, ROGER PEARSON campaign against SWAPO (South West African People's Organization), the Black majority party, in elections held in the fall of 1989. A spokesman for the ethnic organization said, "If we whites were to fight, the whole world would cry because whites are fighting blacks. If it's blacks fighting blacks, no one will care." The same spokesman predicted guerrilla warfare by a "group of black rebels from outside the country" if SWAPO came to power.[189]

Coors has had a national effect with its support for groups whose policies perpetuate the racist divisions in the United States. The Heritage Foundation, for instance, in 1983 advocated repeal of affirmative action policies, reduced enforcement of voting rights and civil rights law, and lessened legal redress for victims of racist actions. Of civil rights law enforcement, the Heritage proposal stated, "The prospect of a bureaucracy forever second-guessing the decisions made by Americans in employment, education and housing is frightening."[190]

In 1981, the Heritage Foundation's *Mandate for Leadership* offered nearly two dozen proposals for reducing or eliminating laws and regulations that combat racist discrimination. One proposal called for the U.S. Justice Department to file amicus briefs "opposing any effort by a private party to obtain equitable relief requiring any form of preferential treatment for any minority group. . ." Also suggested was the banning of racial or sexual employment statistics in corporate annual reports, or the use of "affirmative action employer" in employee recruitment advertising. Even as Heritage claimed to be deregulating business in other areas, it suggested new regulations to prevent corporations from maintaining nondiscrimination policies.[191]

In 1978, the IRS issued a rule that Christian schools could lose their tax exempt status if they were found to engage in racially discriminatory practices. In response, Robert Billings, a board member of the Free Congress Foundation, established the National Christian Action Coalition (NCAC) to lobby for maintaining the tax exemption (in effect, a taxpayer subsidy) for the segregated schools. Billings, the co-founder and first executive director of Moral Majority, was a holder of B.A. and M.A. degrees from Bob Jones University. Bob Jones would stand as an example of segregationist Christian schools. It had long barred African-Americans from admission, and forbade interracial dating among its students.[192]

Billings joined the incoming Reagan Administration's Department of Education in 1981, where he used his post as a "bully pulpit" in the campaign against the IRS policy. In 1982, the Reagan Administration reversed the 1978 IRS rule, reinstating the tax exempt privilege for racially-exclusive schools. In 1983, the Supreme Court overturned that action, and Bob Jones lost its tax exempt status. Jerry Falwell joined the Moon-controlled Coalition for Religious Freedom, which sought to regain Bob Jones' tax exempt status and to get Moon out of jail, where he was serving time for tax fraud and perjury. Falwell and other New Right leaders attended what the *Washington Post* called "a welcome home party for Moon."[193]

Weyrich himself opposed the efforts to end segregation, which he attacked in a 1982 book, *The New Right Papers:* "Culturally destructive government policies—racial hiring quotas and busing come to mind as examples—are to the New Right more immediately important in the realm of action, since the damage they can do is enormous and practically irremediable." This rhetoric sounds dangerously close to some racial theories propounded by racialist and white supremacist groups in the U.S. today. It is noteworthy that the book, *The New Right Papers*, is edited by Robert Whitaker, who was active in the Kanawha County textbook censorship campaign with its racist undercurrents, and in South Boston anti-busing activities, where the racism was more overt.[194]

Whitaker's associate in the Kanawha textbook censorship and South Boston anti-busing campaigns, Robert Hoy, was meeting with nationalist groups influenced by national socialism, and he later praised various neo-Nazi nationalist movements in *Spotlight*, an anti-Semitic newspaper controlled by the quasi-Nazi Liberty Lobby in Washington, D.C. Hoy's photographic essays and articles for *Spotlight* have praised neo-Nazi skinhead groups, the fascist National Front in Great Britain, and other similar groups. Hoy also contributed an essay to *The New Right Papers*, where he called for "seizing the time" to make a right-wing "revolution," noting that Americans had "made one revolution in 1775. If no alternatives are offered, they can make another one today."[195]

Weyrich has also worked with Canadian racist and anti-Semitic elements. Several years ago he spoke at a forum sponsored by Paul Fromm, a leader of the Canadian branch of WACL and a founder of the Western Guard, a Canadian neo-Nazi group.[196]

The Coors political network, including the Heritage Foundation and the Free Congress Foundation, have offered no means of eliminating racism. Its leaders have associated themselves instead with racist elements, as evidenced by the Heritage role in Kanawha County, and by Heritage's continuing association with racialist Roger Pearson. Former Heritage chairman Ben Blackburn of Georgia was even an advocate in the 1970's of literacy tests to limit voting rights.

One of the key activists working with the Reagan Justice Department to dismantle civil rights protections in the mid-1980's was James McClellan, a former aide to Jesse Helms and a top associate of racialist Roger Pearson. McClellan also runs the Center for Judicial Studies and participated in a Free Congress Foundation conference on criminal justice (with Rushdoony) in 1983. While he was working with those inside the Justice

Department to end civil rights protection, he was receiving funding support from the Coors Foundation.[197]

The Coors Foundation also gave $2500 in 1981 to the ultra-rightist Patriotic American Youth, Inc., a group which also distributes explicitly racist literature. The masthead of their related publication mailed from Jackson, Mississippi included names of figures active in the segregationist Citizen's Councils and the Ku Klux Klan. Also active with the group was Judge Tom Brady, whose efforts inspired the formation of the segregationist Citizen's Councils in the 1950's to oppose the 1954 Supreme Court decision striking down the concept of separate but equal in *Brown v. Board of Education*.[198]

THE COORS FAMILY AND CHICANOS

The first call for a boycott of Coors products came in 1966 from Chicano organizations in Colorado. As was the case in other major cities around the country, a white majority police force in Denver was using strong-arm methods to keep minorities contained within ghettos. In New York, Newark, Detroit, and Chicago, for instance, police exercised arbitrary authority and deadly force, instilling fear among the Black populations in those cities. In Denver, the police maintained a heavy presence in the Chicano community.[199]

In the early 1960's, the Coors family aided that presence by donating a helicopter to the Denver police. Local activists charge the helicopter was destined to be used for intrusive surveillance of the Chicano community, and the donation was widely perceived by the Chicano community and its allies as a hostile act of the Coors family toward Chicanos.[200]

In 1966, Joe Coors was installed as a regent of the University of Colorado. He became known for his advocacy of repressing campus dissent and for distributing John Birch Society literature to his fellow regents at their meetings. Activists claim Coors also sought to abolish Chicano and Black studies programs at the University, and to curtail admissions of low-income students because he believed such students would lower academic standards.[201]

Admission of Chicanos to Coors employment was also very low at the time. Although the employment figures have improved since then, Chicano employment (like Black employment) in executive levels barely exists outside the public relations offices. Some of Coors' commitments to improve its ties to the Hispanic business community were called into question in a Hispanic business publication in 1987. Other Hispanic businessmen have brought lawsuits charging Coors with violating or reneging on agree-

While the Coors Corporation goes out of its way to promote its activities in the Black and Chicano communities, *Hispanic Business* magazine has reported charges by Coors critics that this is primarily a public relations ploy. ADOLPH COORS COMPANY, CORPORATE COMMUNICATIONS.

ments with them, agreements that were originally reached to improve Coors' image.[202]

Another development that involves Coors and the Chicano community is that of the English Only campaign. The campaign led a successful fight to pass a state referendum making English the official language of Colorado. Activists fear it could be used to curtail the use of languages other than English in a way that would limit access to state reports, court documents, and other official records by persons who do not read English and who rely on translators and/or materials currently available in Spanish or other non-English editions.

Neither the Coors Corporation nor individual members of the Coors family took any official position on the referendum, according to a Coors statement in 1987. However, leaders of the national campaign do belong to groups which have been funded by Coors. Also, Denver activist Rita Montero, who challenged the ballot status of the referendum in court, found that Joe Coors signed a petition to put the Colorado English Only referendum on the ballot.[203]

The pattern of the Coors Corporation and Foundation giving money to African-American and Chicano civil rights groups for marketing purposes, while funding and serving on the boards of anti-civil rights organizations such as the Heritage Foundation and Free Congress Foundation, was repeated on the English Only issue. While Coors family members did not publicly support the English Only initiative, Coors family funds support groups which actively oppose bilingualism and democratic pluralism.

The national campaign for English Only has several sources of support. One is the parent organization of the Denver-based North-South Institute, formerly known as the Inter-American Security Educational Institute—Denver (ISEI-Denver). The Denver group is an affiliate of the national organization, which is a 501(c)(3) arm of the Moon-connected Council for Inter-American Security (CIS). In short, the North-South Institute is effectively the local affiliate of the CIS. A number of leaders of CIS are also members of the Council for National Policy along with Joe and Holly Coors.[204]

The North-South Institute (NSI) sponsored a program in 1986 where NSI vice-president and director General Gordon Sumner (who is also chair of the national CIS) declared that the conflicts in Latin America could be attributed to the mixture of Spanish culture and Aztec culture. "The mixture has turned into some things that are very unpleasant," Sumner told the audience. When asked about that remark at a 1988 NSI event, Sumner explained that Spanish culture created the Inquisition and Aztec culture practiced human sacrifice, and concluded, "Somehow this combination makes a very violent reaction."[205]

Co-sponsor of this event with NSI was the Independence Institute, which has a cooperative relationship with NSI. The Independence Institute's executive director, John Andrews, also serves on NSI's board. The Independence Institute is located in Golden, Colorado and receives major funding from the Coors Foundation. William Coors was a director of Independence Institute until 1989 and Heritage senior vice-president Burton Yale Pines is, in 1991, still a director. Independence Institute operates as a mini-Heritage Foundation for Colorado issues as well as national and foreign policy issues.[206]

In 1985, the CIS published an alarmist document, On Creating a Hispanic America: A Nation Within a Nation?, which argued that bilingual education programs "could feed and guide terrorism in the United States." The CIS tried to mobilize sentiment against bilingual education, and has tried to link support of bilingual education to "separatism, cultural apartheid and the potential for terrorism in the U.S."[207]

The CIS has been a key New Right group supporting the Contras and right-wing dictatorships in Latin America. It has been part of the

World Anti-Communist League (WACL) since at least 1975, and has strong ties to Moon's Unification Church as well. Contra leader Adolpho Calero, WACL leader Major General John Singlaub, as well as persons with intelligence agency backgrounds, are on the CIS speakers bureau. CIS advocates repressive policies toward Spanish-speaking peoples at home and abroad. The CIS/ISEI boards and key staff are almost exclusively European-Americans.[208]

The CIS is connected to its own anti-foreign language group, English First. The secretary to the CIS board, Larry Pratt, is the president of English First. He also lists himself as president of the American Society of Local Officials, which is chaired by Paul Weyrich and operates out of the offices of the Free Congress Foundation. The American Society of Local Officials has been funded by Coors. Pratt also represents Gun Owners of America, which lobbies for private ownership of machine guns. The English First officers, led by Pratt, are also the officers of United States Border Control, which sends out fundraising letters warning of Mexican welfare fraud, unwed mothers, drugs, and "terrible diseases."[209]

Another effort by an organization tied to groups which Coors supports is a group called U.S. English, run by Dr. John Tanton, a Michigan ophthalmologist. Tanton also founded the anti-immigrant Federation for American Immigration Reform (FAIR), a group that receives funding from the racialist Pioneer Fund, which was run by Tom Ellis, a former president of the Council for National Policy. FAIR's goal was to keep immigrants out of the U.S., while U.S. English's anti-Spanish campaign would make life more difficult and discouraging for those who did come to the United States. In California, recently arrived Asian peoples were also adversely affected.[210]

The largely non-Hispanic, anti-Chicano network of Coors, Independence Institute, North-South Institute, and CIS has already spread views hostile to immigrants from Latin America and to Spanish-speaking peoples in the United States. They have aided in the chauvinistic English Only campaign, which has placed concrete burdens on Spanish-speaking families. And through these networks and others, Coors has aided the Contras, right-wing dictatorships, and even leaders of death squads in Latin America.

THE COORS FAMILY AND THE CONTRAS

When the Reagan Administration began organizing the Nicaraguan Contras in 1981, allied but nominally private groups were formed to build support for the Contra plans.

One of those groups, formed shortly after the first Reagan inauguration, was the U.S. Council for World Freedom (USCWF), headed by Major

General John Singlaub. The USCWF quickly became the U.S. branch of the World Anti-Communist League (WACL). The USCWF began building support for the Reagan policy of aiding not only the Nicaraguan Contras but RENAMO and UNITA in southern Africa and rightist Islamic fundamentalists in Afghanistan. Singlaub informed Central Intelligence Agency director William Casey and National Security Council staff of his actions and operated with their assent, if not under their direction.[211]

One of the early USCWF financial backers was Joe Coors, according to two former USCWF treasurers. Coors shared Reagan's enthusiasm for the Contras despite early indications of the unsavory background of certain Contra leaders and reliable reports of Contra acts of brutality.[212] The Contras were originally known as the 15th of September Legion. Their earliest training came from Argentinian military intelligence, which ran death squads in that country and sponsored a Latin American conference of death squad leaders in 1980. That death squad network was also the Latin American branch of WACL. In 1982, Argentinian intelligence worked with Moon's Unification Church and fugitive Nazi Klaus Barbie to establish a Nazi-style state in Bolivia.[213]

Reliable international monitoring groups have reported that the Contras killed thousands of peasants, slaughtered cattle, and created terror in an apparent effort to undermine the confidence of the Nicaraguan people in their government. Contra project officers in Washington created a covert financial support apparatus run by Oliver North and his superiors. A public financial support apparatus coordinated by Singlaub was also tied into the White House. Joe Coors worked with both fundraising networks.

Joe Coors was one of the boosters of a big fundraising dinner for the Contras in 1985 arranged by the Nicaraguan Refugee Fund at which Reagan was the keynote speaker. The Fund was set up by the Contras' fundraising arm and promoted by a public relations firm whose founder had long-standing Central Intelligence Agency links.[214]

Coors also contributed to the Nicaraguan Freedom Foundation (NFF), established by the Moon-owned *Washington Times*. Board members of NFF included Jeane Kirkpatrick, William Simon, and Michael Novak. Simon and Novak were on the board of PRODEMCA, which also funneled money to the Contras. Jeane Kirkpatrick and her husband Evron Kirkpatrick publish a quarterly magazine, *World Affairs*, which has published an article endorsing the use of death squads.[215]

The Christian Broadcast Network (CBN), whose Regent University is supported by the Coors Foundation and has Holly Coors on its board, was one of the largest donors to the Contra cause, giving millions of dollars to the Contras in Central America (the Nicaraguan Freedom Foundation funds went there as well). Christian Broadcast Network owner Pat

Joe Coors was an early financial backer of the U.S. Council for World Freedom, the U.S. affiliate of the World Anti-Communist League (WACL). WACL helped coordinate Contra fundraising while networking reactionary, fascist, and Nazi-collaborationist forces worldwide.

UNITED STATES COUNCIL FOR WORLD FREEDOM, *INTELLIGENCE BRIEFING,* FALL 1988.

Robertson held a telethon on May 30, 1985 to raise funds for the Contras.[216]

Another active Contra support group was Citizens for America, co-chaired by Lewis Lehrman and Holly Coors. Citizens for America was formed in coordination with the White House in 1983 to build support for Reagan's programs. In 1985, it organized a tour of twenty Contras to two hundred congressional districts to lobby for Contra funding. Lehrman also organized a June 2, 1985 meeting in Angola that brought together the Nicaraguan Contras, the South African-backed UNITA leaders, and similar rightist groups from around the world.[217]

Other Coors-funded groups that have actively supported the Contras include the Heritage Foundation, the Free Congress Foundation, and the Conservative Caucus (TCC). TCC has said, for example, "The Conservative Caucus has advocated a strategy of victory over Communism in Nicaragua from the very beginning—and we will continue to press for aid to the Contras, de-recognition of the Sandinistas . . . and a new government, friendly to the United States." [218]

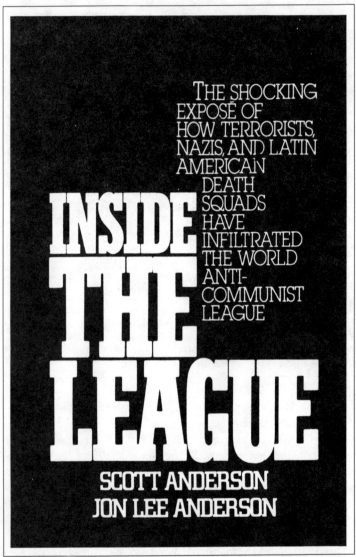

THE SHOCKING
EXPOSÉ OF
HOW TERRORISTS,
NAZIS, AND LATIN
AMERICAN
DEATH
SQUADS
HAVE
INFILTRATED
THE WORLD
ANTI-
COMMUNIST
LEAGUE

INSIDE THE LEAGUE

SCOTT ANDERSON
JON LEE ANDERSON

Inside the League chronicled how "Terrorists, Nazis, and Latin American Death Squads" had infiltrated the World Anti-Communist League (WACL). Joe Coors was a major financial backer of WACL's U.S. affiliate, led by Major General John Singlaub, USA (ret).

SCOTT ANDERSON AND JON LEE ANDERSON, *INSIDE THE LEAGUE*
(NEW YORK: DODD, MEAD & CO., 1986).

Joe Coors also became involved with Oliver North in the clandestine Contra support networks. On May 21, 1987, he told Congress that he met with Central Intelligence Agency director William Casey, on June 18, 1985, to offer support for the Contras. (Coors knew Casey from the 1980 presidential campaign and had been funding the National Strategy Information Center with which Casey had worked.) Casey directed Coors to Oliver North, who got Coors to buy a small airplane for the Contras. Coors then transferred $65,000 from his account to the Lake Resources account in Switzerland controlled by North.[219]

The Heritage Foundation was also involved in the secret Contra funding schemes. Heritage in 1985 "donated" $100,000 to the Institute for North-South Issues (INSI), an Oliver North-connected conduit. From INSI, $80,000 of the money went to the account of I.C., Inc., a North-Spitz Channell conduit to the Contras. The $100,000 came from a private contributor contacted by Roy Godson, a National Security Council consultant and director of the National Strategy Information Center. A Congressional report noted, "The true objective of this 'grant' was disguised in correspondence between (Richard) Miller (as Treasurer of INSI) and Edwin J. Feulner (as president of Heritage Foundation) with whom Godson had met previously."[220]

The "private" aid that Coors and others provided to the Contras appeared to violate U.S. neutrality laws which state:

> Whoever, within the United States, knowingly begins or sets on foot [sic] or provides or prepares a means for or furnishes the money for, or takes part in, any military or naval expedition or enterprise to be carried on from thence against the territory or dominion of any foreign prince or state, or of any colony, district, or people with whom the United States is at peace, shall be fined not more than $3,000 or imprisoned not more than three years, or both.[221]

In fact, several other private individuals supplying aid to the Contras have been prosecuted. Spitz Channell and members of Civilian Military Assistance, for example, have been indicted for the violation of federal laws. In 1985, Jack Terrel, a leader of a civilian commando unit that aided the Contras and himself indicted in the Iran-Contra scandal, revealed that "Coors brewery is one of the Contras' biggest supporters."[222]

THE COORS FAMILY AND ORGANIZED LABOR

❝ *I honestly see very little appropriate role for unions*
in this day and age. **❞**

Joe Coors
The Nation
APRIL 15, 1978, p. 434

On April 12, 1977 the AFL-CIO called for a boycott of Coors beer, supporting a call by Brewery Workers Local 366 on April 5, 1977 for such a boycott. The local's strike was strongly motivated by non-economic human rights issues. Coors employees claimed that Joe Coors was so contemptuous of his employees that he called them "monkeys." In the Discipline and Discharge section of the contract in force prior to the strike was language that permitted the firing of employees for "disrespect toward superiors; disparaging remarks about the employer or the employer's products, or any words or deeds which would discourage any person from drinking Coors beer."[223]

In spite of Coors' pro-family rhetoric, when it came to families of Coors workers, their needs were ignored for the sake of production. Instead of being allowed to work straight shifts, employees were forced to work swing shifts, in spite of a 1974 vote that expressed preference for the straight shift. On occasion, shift assignments were changed daily.

Foremost among the human dignity issues, however, was Coors' use of lie detectors when hiring or investigating employees. Coors claimed that such methods were needed to protect the Coors family from malevolent employees. Questions were routinely asked about a prospective employee's political orientation and sexual habits. Critics charged these tests were designed to weed out persons on the basis of their political views or sexual preference, although the Coors Corporation has denied this charge.[224]

As the local *Rocky Mountain News* editorialized, "A lie detector carries only one message to an employee: It says the company does not trust an employee's word. It is a personal insult. . .that [treads] heavily into privacy and Fifth Amendment rights under the Constitution." Noting the intransigence of Coors on this issue, the *News* noted that corporations are not obligated to sign contracts, but only to bargain in good faith, "So unions are vulnerable. They can be busted by companies that negotiate but do not sign."[225]

The history of Coors' union-busting is indeed a long one. An undated AFL-CIO statement noted that "The Coors company has destroyed nineteen unions since 1960, including the Boilermakers, Ironworkers, Electricians and Plumbers and Pipefitters locals. In each case the company would propose an outrageous 'final offer,' thus forcing a strike. Coors would then hire non-union replacements and conduct a decertification election with a majority scab workforce."[226]

Following its historical practice, Coors began seeking removal of the Brewers union in 1977. It began demanding open shop language in the contract after the strike began. The day after the strike began, Coors sent letters to each employee threatening that:

> If it is necessary to replace striking employees in order to maintain our operations, we shall do so. Accordingly, we feel that it is only fair to inform you that in the event you are permanently replaced, you may lose your position with this Company.

Within a couple of weeks, a number of strikers returned to work. Coors hired hundreds of non-union workers to continue operations.[227]

Following familiar union-busting procedures, Coors called for a decertification election among the non-striking employees, without striking union supporters being eligible to vote. The decertification election was held after delays, on December 14 and 15, 1978. Some months prior to the election, Coors family members called for the abolition of Local 366. Peter Coors, one of the supposedly more moderate sons of Joe Coors, told the *Rocky Mountain News* that there was little chance of settling labor disputes unless workers left Local 366. Coors won the decertification election, ending Local 366's role as bargaining agent. The national AFL-CIO boycott continued.[228]

In a 1981 letter to AFL-CIO Secretary-Treasurer Thomas Donahue, William Coors wrote, "If and when the dust ever settles on this conflict, I give you my personal guarantee that the AFL-CIO will have spilled one hundred times more blood than we. If you would ever bother to do your homework, you would learn that you can only get to a part of us, and we can get all of you." Coors said that the AFL-CIO was attempting to destroy his company and referred to the union official as "my self-appointed executioner." Coors signed the letter, "Disgustedly yours." Donahue responded that "to read your statements swearing vengeance against the AFL-CIO over a fight you started, seems to me more ideological than practical."[229]

Ideological anti-union militancy has long been present at Coors. During the strike of the United Farm Workers in the 1960's, Coors trucks were used to haul non-union grapes, and William Coors promised to buy these grapes to give to his friends. As in other social matters, members of the Coors family amplify their views with money and organizational involvement.[230]

There are a number of well-funded groups whose policies, if implemented, would cripple unionism in this country. Foremost among them is the National Right to Work Committee (NRTWC), headed by Reed Larson, a member of the Council for National Policy. The NRTWC is supported by corporations and individuals such as Coors. The NRTWC has refused to identify its corporate supporters. The Coors family has supported the anti-union group through the use of corporate funds, the family foundation, and personal checks.[231]

In his 1981 letter to the AFL-CIO's Donahue, William Coors also noted that the Council for a Union-Free Environment (CUFE) and the United States Industrial Council (USIC) were supporting Coors, making the company a "cause celebre." What Coors could have also noted is that he is personally active in USIC and the Coors family is a funder of USIC.[232]

The United States Industrial Council was founded in 1933 as the Southern States Industrial Council to oppose policies of the New Deal. Formerly based in Nashville, Tennessee, it now operates out of a Washington, D.C. office and is run by Anthony Harrigan, a denizen of the far right whose affiliations include the American Security Council. The USIC has several thousand member corporations and is to the right of the National Association of Manufacturers, the high council of American industry, in which Coors has also been active.[233]

Coors' commitment toward safe working conditions for employees was called into question in 1984 as a result of investigations of two deaths and an injury to Coors' workers in 1982. Coors' record on worker safety was also illustrated by its resistance to federal safety inspections. Government officials have claimed Coors used political influence to reduce federal oversight of working conditions at Coors. On September 2, 1982, an employee was overcome by toxic fumes despite her use of a respirator with an outside air supply. Two employees who tried to rescue her died from the fumes. Two others were also injured. Coors was fined only $810.[234]

In the years immediately preceding Reagan's inauguration, Coors had been subject to over twenty plant inspections in a thirty-three month period. After Reagan became president, the rate dropped to only four in a thirty-two month period. Three of those four investigations were prompted by fatalities at the Coors plant in 1982.[235]

The Coors company often complained about safety inspections by the federal Occupational Safety and Health Administration (OSHA). As a matter of policy, Coors refused to allow OSHA inspectors access to its plants without a search warrant. A former assistant regional director for the Denver office, Harry Borchelt, testified that the OSHA headquarters in Washington "was very interested in what we were doing at Coors." He said that the scrutiny was due to the close ties between Coors family members

The Heritage Lectures 12

The Political Future of American Trade Unions

John Burton

The Heritage Foundation

Below:
Reed Larson heads the militantly anti-union National Right to Work Committee, a group supported by the Coors family, foundation, and corporation.

COUNCIL FOR NATIONAL POLICY, MEETING PROGRAM, FEBRUARY 1989, ORLANDO, FLORIDA.

Above:
The Coors family funded Heritage Foundation published this study which warned of the increased political activity of trade unions and speculated that unions might use "the Democratic Party as its Trojan Horse within the established American political party system."

HERITAGE FOUNDATION, UNDATED, CIRCA 1981.

and Reagan and that local inspectors felt pressured to give special consideration to Coors.[236]

When OSHA drew up a national rating of thousands of companies based on likely accident rates, several Coors companies scored badly. OSHA used a scale ranging from one to thirty-six. A score of one indicated the most dangerous companies. Of over one hundred Denver-area companies, only the Coors' two porcelain plants rated a one, indicating the highest possible accident rate. The Coors Container Company was rated a seven. Shortly thereafter, Coors arranged a luncheon meeting with several key OSHA figures, including the deputy assistant secretary Mark Cowan. In a letter to Cowan, who was a conservative activist, a Coors official complained about the OSHA regional director, Curtis Foster. Although the letter mentioned an incident that occurred over three years previously, the Coors official wrote, "Hopefully, you will be able to correct future occurrences of this type of behavior." Shortly thereafter, Foster was fired on an unrelated issue. Foster filed an administrative protest and was reinstated three years later. Coors insisted it applied no pressure to have him fired.[237]

The AFL-CIO and Coors came to an agreement on August 19, 1987, whereby the company agreed to a prompt secret ballot election and other concessions, while the union federation agreed to end its boycott. The AFL-CIO eventually conceded to the Teamsters the right to organize the brewery workers. In late 1988, the Coors family personally campaigned against the unionization vote on the eve of the election. The company spent just under $50,000 on the anti-union "Keep Coors Yours" campaign. Again the Coors family won the vote. Lately, Coors has been experimenting with quality circles, as well as Japanese team concepts. Such methods may provide an outlet for employee dissatisfaction and help short-circuit any future union organizing attempts.[238]

THE COORS FAMILY AND THE ENVIRONMENT

As environmental concerns increased in the 1960's and 1970's, Congress passed legislation to preserve disappearing wilderness areas, prevent air and water pollution, and limit hazardous and destructive industrial and agricultural practices. These measures often conflicted with the prevailing practices of industrial, agribusiness, and ranching interests. The Adolph Coors Company was one of those businesses that decided to fight the environmental movement politically and to challenge environmental regulations in court. Led by Joe Coors, who *Reader's Digest* called "one of the country's leading anti-environmentalists," the Coors Company bankrolled organizations and individuals that wanted to destroy or minimize environmental protection legislation. This network extended into the Reagan Administration after the 1980 elections.[239]

The Coors corporation has many activities and operations that are affected by environmental policy. For the manufacture of beer, thousands of acres are used to grow barley, rice, and hops which are brewed with millions of gallons of fresh water each year. Tons of waste must be discarded. Additionally, the Adolph Coors Company has subsidiaries involved in oil drilling and pumping, coal mining, and cattle. For corporations, the financial advantage of minimizing environmental regulation is obvious, and may have less to do with abstract *laissez-faire* economics than with a diversified conglomerate seeking to exploit the environment without paying the costs.

Putting money into the Heritage Foundation, which advocated reduced governmental regulation on environmental matters, simply wasn't enough. Coors and other wealthy Western business interests were inspired by a novel idea from the California Chamber of Commerce. The Chamber had founded the Pacific Legal Foundation in 1973 to bring lawsuits on behalf of the business community as "public interest" actions. Coors and others took the idea and created the pro-business National Legal Center for the Public Interest. With Joe Coors on its board and with Coors funds, the National Legal Center sought to create multi-state, regional legal groups modeled on the California group. Coors consultant (and later vice-president) John T. McCarty was also a director of the National Legal Center. In 1976, the National Legal Center put up $50,000 and Coors put up $25,000 to create the Mountain States Legal Foundation (MSLF) in Denver. Coors consultant Clifford Rock, who helped Coors start the Heritage Foundation, did the initial fundraising and organizational work for Mountain States.[240]

James Watt was hired in mid-1977 as MSLF's first president. Joe Coors had met him in 1975 at a National Legal Center reception in Washington, D.C. Holly Coors had known Watt since 1975 through A Christian Ministry in the National Parks, a group that continues to receive support from the Coors Foundation. With Coors' approval, Watt set out to implement the legal agenda of his corporate backers. MSLF immediately filed friend-of-the-court briefs opposing an affirmative action program at the University of Colorado Law School, seeking to limit health and safety inspections of businesses, and arguing for the repeal of Idaho's ratification of the Equal Rights Amendment. As MSLF's funding soared, Watt began to initiate lawsuits on behalf of his corporate sponsors. One writer summarized Watt's legal actions thus: "The Foundation [MSLF] went to court to block lower utility rates for the elderly in Colorado and Utah, arguing successfully that these 'lifeline' rates would discriminate against other customers. The Foundation tackled such enemies of western business interests as the Environmental Protection Agency, the Sierra Club, the Environmental Defense

Fund—and the Department of the Interior. In the process the organization picked up the reputation of being anti-consumer, anti-feminist, anti-government, anti-Black, and above all, anti-environmentalist."[241]

In MSLF's first year, Joe Coors gave $85,000 to the foundation, according to MSLF internal documents obtained by investigative writer Jeff Stein. Oil companies such as Phillips, Amoco, and Marathon kicked in much of the rest of the early funding. The budget grew from $194,000 in 1977 to $1.2 million in 1980, with additional support from Chevron, Shell, western utilities, and others directly affected by environmental regulations.[242]

MSLF maintains a "board of litigation," as well as a corporate board of directors. The board of litigation is composed of attorneys who plan the group's legal actions. This prevents MSLF's corporate directors from appearing to dictate the initiation of lawsuits to serve their personal business interests. The clients of the attorneys on the board of litigation, however, include the oil companies, utilities, and other businesses backing MSLF.

Jeffrey H. Coors was chairman of the Free Congress Foundation when it co-published with the Heritage Foundation *Issues '88: A Platform for America* which contained policy recommendations for the incoming Bush Administration. Among the suggestions was gutting federal oversight of the environment "through innovative policies which replace bureaucratic plodding with aggressive free market incentives."

FREE CONGRESS FOUNDATION, ANNUAL REPORT, 1988.

Further, reporter Stein found through access to internal memos that Watt had co-authored a memo tying the board of litigation to MSLF's corporate sponsors. The memo also expressed concern about the Carter Administration's plans to designate certain lands as wilderness areas, which would prevent them from being mined, drilled, or developed on a major scale. In the memo, Watt asked affected corporate members of MSLF to meet with his board of directors and the board of litigation and discuss a lawsuit against the wilderness plan which would "benefit the entire private sector." MSLF's stated purpose is to benefit the *public* sector.[243]

A second area of Coors anti-environmentalist work was in the state legislature of Colorado. Coors supported the campaigns of Anne Gorsuch Burford and other Republicans known for their "unconventional legislative tactics and extreme anti-government regulation views." Burford, who also socialized with Joe Coors, joined efforts with Watt and James Sanderson to "stop measures in the legislature giving the state authority to regulate toxic substances and to begin a program for the disposal of toxic wastes." Sanderson was an attorney who worked for Coors and MSLF.[244]

With the inauguration of Reagan in 1981, what *The New York Times* called a "Colorado Mafia" backed by Coors took over the key offices regulating national environmental matters. James Watt became Secretary of the Interior, while Anne Gorsuch Burford (then Anne Gorsuch) was selected to head the Environmental Protection Agency (EPA). Another legislative colleague of Anne Gorsuch Burford, Robert Burford (later her husband), was a wealthy rancher with 32,000 acres of grazing permits on Bureau of Land Management (BLM) territory. He was a leader of efforts to destroy the BLM, a part of the Department of the Interior. Watt gave him the directorship of the BLM.[245]

Coors had many avenues to make sure that its waste disposal needs were known to the EPA. Anne Gorsuch Burford brought Sanderson and another Coors attorney, Thornton Field, to EPA as consultants, while another right-wing colleague from the Colorado legislature, Steven Durham, was made EPA director for the six-state region that included Colorado. Thornton Field, the Coors attorney who was also a consultant to EPA, advised Anne Gorsuch Burford specifically on hazardous waste matters. Field had been a Coors lobbyist and had worked with Burford when she was a legislator, successfully stopping efforts to close down an industrial waste dump. All were in positions to help the Adolph Coors Company with permission to dump waste in ways that many thought were hazardous to the health of area residents.[246] In 1982, the Coors network in Washington and Denver maneuvered to reopen temporarily a landfill to give Coors and other corporations an opportunity to rid themselves of waste materials. Before the dumpsite was closed, Coors had disposed of an estimated twenty million gallons of toxic liquid wastes at the dumpsite known as the Lowry Landfill. Nearby groundwater was contaminated from the landfill to such an extent that Lowry was being considered for cleanup under the Superfund program which targets the most contaminated sites in the country.[247]

Instead of seeking alternative waste disposal sites, the Coors crowd manipulated the regulations to allow further dumping at Lowry. The landfill was managed by a Chicago-area firm, Chemical Waste Management, which was a client of James Sanderson, the EPA consultant who also worked for Coors. Sanderson arranged for Steven Durham to lift the no-dumping ban at Lowry for two weeks in 1982. Durham even advised the waste company to begin moving drums of liquid toxic wastes to the dumpsite because a lifting of the dumping ban was "anticipated." Another EPA memo suggested that Durham bring the rule change "to the attention of such companies as Conoco, Coors, Martin Marietta, Hewlett-Packard."[248]

An estimated forty-six drums of waste from Coors were stored at the burial site just before the ban was temporarily lifted. Coors had been disposing of such liquids as lead dross (from can manufacturing), flammable solvents, and cyanide solution. Congressional committees found that EPA knew that the landfill operator, Chemical Waste Management, kept two sets of books to conceal leaks at the dump. One EPA staffer told the *National Catholic Reporter* that the Lowry landfill situation was "a case of shady deals being worked out between EPA people, Coors people, and Chemical Waste."[249]

When the incoming Reagan Administration was looking for a Secretary of the Interior, their first choice was not James Watt but former Wyoming Governor Cliff Hansen. When Hansen declined the job, he suggested James Watt to the Reagan recruiters. Joe Coors immediately approved the idea, got the support of Senator Paul Laxalt, and Watt quickly became Reagan's nominee.[250]

Watt became a major source of controversy: he began selling off public lands to developers, giving mining and oil interests access to ecologically sensitive public lands, wildlife refuges, and parks, and he began expanding oil drilling on the outer shelf. From the beginning of his Cabinet tenure in 1981, Watt advocated policies which were unpopular with much of the public; he was frequently criticized in the media.

In 1982, the Free Congress Research and Education Foundation initiated a project (it was Weyrich's idea) to produce a book that would counter critics of Watt and present Watt in a more "balanced" way. Ron Arnold wrote *At the Eye of the Storm: James Watt and the Environmentalists* and in it found no substantive reason to criticize "Jim" (as the book often referred to Watt). Instead, Arnold argued that environmentalists are insidious totalitarians who are "anti-technology, anti-civilization, anti-humanity." These adjectives, and his attacks on some environmentalists as drug pushers, bear an uncanny resemblance to the propaganda of the neo-Nazi Lyndon LaRouche. Arnold's book even cites a LaRouche follower as a source for some allegations of drug ties to environmentalism. LaRouche met with Watt in 1981 after Watt became Secretary of the Interior and former LaRouche group members have claimed that Watt nearly hired LaRouche as a consultant. Watt has stated, however, that he felt instinctively that "something was off" with LaRouche.[251]

The Coors Foundation has funded Arnold's Center for the Defense of Free Enterprise, in Bellevue, Washington. In recent years, Arnold's group has shared officers and directors with the American Freedom Coalition, the political arm of Sun Myung Moon's Unification Church discussed earlier. In turn, Arnold is the registered agent for the American Freedom Coalition in the state of Washington. Arnold told a Canadian newspaper, "The Center for the Defense of Free Enterprise is allied in a movement [with the Unification Church] but has no affiliation with it in terms of money exchange."[252]

The anti-environmental character of the Coors network is also reflected in the Heritage Foundation's recommendations for the Interior Department and the Environmental Protection Agency. In its 1981 book, *Mandate for Leadership*, Heritage declared that the Carter Administration "displayed zealotry" in its restrictions on surface mining for coal. It called for a long-term review of rules on surface mining to identify those regulations that "unnecessarily burden" coal companies. Of wilderness areas, Heritage suggested, "The new Administration should issue a Solicitor's Opinion revising and clarifying the exploration provisions of the Wilderness Act, declaring that such exploration constitutes the *dominant* use of such lands." (emphasis added) In other areas, such as water policy, Heritage insisted that state law should prevail over federal policy, and that water law in Western states "must remain inviolate." After contributing to the Heritage recommendations, Perry Pendley was named by Watt as his Deputy Assistant Secretary for Energy and Minerals. Another Heritage contributor, Dave Russell, became Deputy Assistant Secretary for Land and Water Resources. In 1983, Heritage continued to advocate corporate access to minerals on public lands but argued for the sale of those lands to developers. [253]

Heritage also recommended "decentralizing" decision-making for the Environmental Protection Agency, "delegating functions to the states and returning decision-making to private individuals." The author of this proposal, Gail Ann Norton, was the senior counsel with the Mountain States Legal Foundation. [254]

If EPA functions and decision-making are left to private individuals such as Joe Coors, and to the states, where right-wing legislators can block environmental protections as Burford did in Colorado, then more Lowry landfills will be the probable result.

THE COORS FAMILY AND THE MEDIA

A s Joe Coors began looking at the national landscape in the early 1970's, he must have realized that sympathetic media outlets were a necessary component of any serious bid for national influence. It was during this time that Spiro Agnew was regularly attacking the national media for an alleged liberal bias. The New Right was concerned that the media was not under its influence. Coors decided to create his own national media outlet.

In May 1973, Coors launched Television News, Inc. (TVN) in New York City as a national feature service for local television news programs. It became the only source of news film for local stations other than the networks. Joe Coors, who told a Denver paper that TVN was to counter "liberal left" network news, soon found the professional staff was producing features incompatible with his right-wing views. He installed as president of TVN Jack Wilson, the same aide who was helping him set up the Heritage Foundation in Washington. Two months after TVN began, Wilson was writing to Coors complaining about TVN coverage of the Reverend Martin Luther King, Jr., "an avowed communist revolutionary." Prior to that, Wilson had gone to Germany without the knowledge of the professional staff to do a news story that was seen as supportive of the leadership of the Christian Democratic Union/Christian Social Union (the latter group headed by Bavarian rightist Franz Josef Strauss, with whom Joe Coors' Washington, D.C. strategist Paul Weyrich maintained a political relationship). At the time, Wilson was on the payroll of the Coors company and was a member of TVN's board of directors. TVN staff refused to use the story.[255]

The Coors-Wilson project faced a dilemma. If TVN got rid of its professional staff, local stations would drop the service. Some were already questioning Coors' motives with TVN, which was losing several million dollars per year.

On the other hand, Coors' need to keep the professional staff meant resistance to broadcasting his political material. Coors had big goals for TVN, including plans for setting up a television transmission network using satellite technology. A report in Columbia Journalism Review noted, "It's an idea that would make TVN first with a dramatic new technology—a plan management hopes will make Coors as big a name in broadcast journalism as it is in beer."

Eventually Jack Wilson fired the news director and took more direct control of TVN news operations. In came Paul Weyrich, George Bush's

1988 image-maker Roger Ailes, and William Kling (who would later join Weyrich's staff). Weyrich was a political adviser to TVN, taking its reporters to meet conservatives such as then-Senator Carl Curtis. Weyrich was then being carried on the Senator's staff so that he could get insurance coverage while working for Heritage, Television News, Inc., and later the Committee for the Survival of a Free Congress. Weyrich also brought TVN news staff together with Ed Feulner and Howard Phillips. Weyrich once wrote the questions a TVN reporter used in an interview with Senator Curtis.[256]

John McCarty, a Coors employee and member of the Heritage Foundation advisory board, joined Wilson to screen potential TVN employees, using what a former TVN news director called a "political litmus test." Wilson served as a Heritage trustee at the time.

Wilson (who forbade reporting on Ralph Nader, Daniel Ellsberg, Native American activists, and followers of the Reverend Martin Luther King, Jr.) wanted TVN to become a "moral cement" for the United States. In a memo to Coors, Wilson discussed changes needed if "this service is to be the force which we expected." He was quoted as saying, "I hate all those network people. They're destroying the country. We have to unify the country."

Of course, challenging the networks is in itself an entirely legitimate

The rightist Accuracy in Media is headed by Reed Irvine, who is not so much a media critic as a reactionary ideologue. Irvine, for instance, told a March 1990 Massachusetts audience that he thought the U.S. government should "take the handcuffs off" the government of El Salvador and authorize the purchase of napalm for use against the FMLN opposition forces.

ACCURACY IN MEDIA
PROMOTIONAL LITERATURE

SOURCE: INSTITUTE FOR EDUCATIONAL AFFAIRS, ANNUAL REPORT, 1989.

The Collegiate Network
Institute For Educational Affairs

Amherst Spectator
Badger Herald
 (U. of Wisconsin)
Binghamton Times
 (SUNY Binghamton)
Boston College Observer
Brandeisian (Brandeis)
Brown Spectator
California Review
 (U.C. Berkeley)
California Review
 (U.C. San Diego)
Campus Review (U. of Iowa)
Carleton Observer
Carolina Critic
 (UNC-Chapel Hill)
Chicago Crucible
 (U. of Chicago)
Claremont Independent
Cornell Review
Dartmouth Review
Dialogue at Notre Dame
Duke Blue
Duke Review
Eli (Yale)
Federalist Paper (Columbia)
Florida Leader
Florida Review (U. of Florida)
Free Thinker (Occidental)
Galenstone (Wellesley)
Georgetown's Blue and Gray
Harvard Salient

Hopkins Spectator
 (Johns Hopkins U.)
Illini Review (U. of Illinois)
Kenyon Observer
Michigan Review
 (Ann Arbor)
Minnesota Spectator
Minuteman
 (U. Mass-Amherst)
Northwestern Review
Oregon Commentator
Perspective (Radford)
Primary Source (Tufts)
Princeton Sentinel
Princeton Tory
Red and Blue
 (U. of Pennsylvania)
Redwood Review
 (UC-Santa Cruz)
Remnant (William and Mary)
Rutgers Free Press
Spartan Review (San Jose St.)
Stanford Review
Texas Review
UWM Times
 (UW-Milwaukee)
Vassar Spectator
Virginia Advocate
Washington Spectator
Wesleyan Review
Williams Observer
Yale Free Press
Yale Political Magazine

The Institute for Educational Affairs funds conservative and reactionary college publications such as the *Dartmouth Review*, a publication which uses phrases such as "used Brillo pad" and "mud pie" to refer to a Black, "wombats" to refer to women, and "fruits, butches and assorted scum" to refer to gay men and lesbians.

activity. The Coors claim of being a professional, balanced news service, however, apparently lacked foundation. Rather than openly state its goals and purpose, TVN's method may be suggested by a statement Wilson made to a news editor: "I'm not sure you understand our philosophy. Do you see that tugboat out there? Did you ever see the way a tugboat turns an ocean liner around? It doesn't do it in one swift motion. It pushes and nudges the liner slowly. That's the way we want to put our philosophy in the news: gradually, subtly, slowly. It must be subtle."

REACTIONARY MEDIA PRESSURE GROUPS

Setting up a potential right-wing news network to counter the television networks was only the beginning of Coors' attempt to reshape media messages. While TVN went out of business in 1975, a group of New Right pressure groups evolved in an attempt to bludgeon national print and electronic media into a rightist posture. Coors became a funder of a number of them, including Morality in Media, the Media Institute, and Accuracy in Media.[257]

The best known among these pressure groups is Accuracy in Media, headed by Reed Irvine in Washington, D.C. The group has been allied with Moon's Unification Church, which has provided volunteer staff to work with Irvine. The Congressional investigation of South Korean Central Intelligence Agency activities in the U.S. in the 1970's found that the KCIA intended to "utilize" AIM to counter North Korean influence and to work in "media circles." [258]

AIM also initiated Accuracy in Academia (AIA), which received national press attention for its plans to spy on university professors. The group, originally headed by Les Csorba, shared the office and phones of AIM. Csorba planned to utilize information from his spies to pressure universities to curb or fire professors of whom AIA disapproved. Csorba has written soliciting support for Accuracy in Academia in the newspaper of the Maranatha shepherding cult, which also promoted the Institute for Educational Affairs.

Csorba was hired by the Bush Administration to work on the religious group and conservative group liaison staff of the White House and later was moved to the personnel office.[259]

The Coors family funds a number of right-wing newspapers through the family foundation. *The American Spectator*, a monthly published just outside of Washington, D.C., has been a recipient of Coors money.[260]

Coors also funds the Institute for Educational Affairs (IEA), a tax exempt group set up in 1978, which funds right-wing campus newspapers. The IEA's 1988 annual report states that they have "been assisting students at scores of American colleges and universities in their efforts to found and publish campus newspapers and magazines." These publications are collectively known as the Collegiate Network. One of these papers, the *Dartmouth Review*, is well-known for using phrases such as "used Brillo pad" and "mud pie" to refer to an African-American, "wombats" to refer to women, and "fruits, butches and assorted scum" to refer to gay men and lesbians. Dartmouth president James Freedman has publicly called the *Dartmouth Review* "irresponsible, mean-spirited, cruel and ugly."[261]

The number of papers in the Collegiate Network (CN) fluctuates, but at the end of 1988 there were forty-one papers. IEA contributed about $100,000 to CN papers and conducts general oversight of the papers. IEA does on-site inspections of each paper, conducts conferences on newspaper operations, and maintains a toll-free hotline for papers to call them with "problems."[262]

To further assist the propagation of these papers, IEA set up a national advertising consortium to sell advertising space for all the papers as a package. The Coors Corporation has bought ads in all the Collegiate Network papers. The IEA also makes grants for conservative research projects and books such as *Red Star Over Tibet*.[263]

The Institute for Educational Affairs is run by Leslie Lenkowsky, a former interim deputy director of the U.S. Information Agency (USIA). In 1984, Lenkowsky was rejected by the Senate for confirmation to a permanent appointment to that position. His rejection was due primarily to the Senate's belief that he was responsible for blacklisting liberal speakers from the USIA's speakers program.[264]

IEA literature does not describe itself as conservative but as supporting "the battle of ideas," and as a group trying to create "a national dialogue about what our guiding principles might be." Its board includes rejected Supreme Court nominee Robert Bork, Heritage President Edwin Feulner, and drug "czar" William Bennett.[265]

In 1986, the IEA formed the Philanthropic Roundtable, a network of over 130 conservative and right-wing foundations and corporations. IEA's stated purpose in creating the Roundtable was "to create a network where innovative ideas could be translated into effective projects for foundations, corporations and individual donors." Innovative ideas, as judged by the Roundtable's projects, are right-wing ideas. The Coors Foundation is a member of the Roundtable.[266]

THE COORS FAMILY AND EDUCATION

The Coors family, primarily through the family's foundation, is tied to a number of conservative and reactionary groups which attack pluralism and public education. The goal of equal access to education for all Americans—once seen as an essential element of a democratic and pluralistic state—has engendered an apprehensive and sometimes hostile response from conservatives. They see the wider distribution of wealth, goods and services, including education, as inimical to their interests or ideology. They will attack a program that seeks to broaden the educational franchise, be it affirmative action or financial aid to low-income students, as diluting or cheapening the education for the preferred few.

Many conservative activists have called for the complete elimination of taxpayer-funded free public education and for the adoption in its place of a free market, *laissez-faire* solution to education. Schools will proliferate, they argue, and the quality of education will improve, when the dominance of the public education system is replaced by the stimulus of an unregulated, free market economy. These private educational companies—with no direct control by local communities—would benefit from various tax plans advocated by the right. Similarly, many conservative organizations opposed to federal and state tax policies focus almost entirely on those taxes that directly support public education and often call for the abolition of all education taxes.

Another focus of the campaign to alter the public education agenda is the attempt to force textbook publishers and school boards to promote rightist ideology in civics, history, and other schoolbooks. These attempts often equate secular public education with a conspiracy by anti-religious, secular humanist, even satanic educators, all determined to undermine traditional American values. Similarly, the issues of prayer in school and the teaching of Biblical "creationism"—the Bible's literal story of Creation instead of evolution studies—provide emotional campaign issues for attempts to dominate school systems and revise local curriculums.

TEXTBOOK CENSORSHIP

In the past ten years, the Coors foundation has contributed more than $130,000 to Educational Research Analysts, incorporated as a non-profit corporation in 1973 and run by Mel and Norma Gabler out of their Longview, Texas home.[267] The Gablers, whose work has been endorsed by such right-wing luminaries as Phyllis Schlafly, Jerry Falwell, and Richard Viguerie, have searched textbooks since 1962 for signs of what they regard as unpatriotic, anti-Christian, or anti-family sentiment. In accordance with Texas policy, they file lists of particular objections to proposed texts and then testify before the state textbook committee on their objections (only publishers are allowed to *defend* their challenged textbooks). In such cases, the Texas Board of Education often balks at purchasing the blacklisted text, to avoid protests stirred-up by the highly-publicized Gablers.

Texas is considered a key state in the establishment of national educational policy because it represents a large portion of the national textbook market and because of its unusual textbook adoption process. Texas selects textbooks on the state level and only books on the state's approved list are eligible for purchase by Texas schools. Since few publishers are willing to lose the lucrative Texas market and because it is seldom financially feasible to produce one textbook for Texas and unexpurgated editions for other states, many publishers avoid topics and views which would trigger the Gablers' objections. Many are also willing to amend their textbooks to meet Texas standards. As a result, the Gablers have the ability to lower the quality of textbooks nationally. Additionally, the Gablers' reviews of educational texts are widely distributed and form the documentation for many local protests. One textbook publisher made the situation clear: "Publishers are very much aware of the Gablers' concerns. We have to walk a narrow line."

The Gablers use the language of the Bible, seen as literally true, as their primary authority in making evaluations of texts. They believe that secular humanism, developed by John Dewey and others in the late nineteenth century, now pervades the American media and educational establishment. They see secular humanism and the values of modernity as engaged in a great battle with Christianity. They believe that Christian viewpoints and values should be integrated into the public school system and that the secular humanist bias they perceive there must be eliminated.

Under this philosophy, a wide range of issues are deeply problematic for the Gablers. For example, because they believe that the Bible condemns socialism and mandates free enterprise, the Gablers object to textbook discussion of the Great Depression on the grounds that it might "raise doubts about our system." Similarly, because the Bible is opposed to "women's liberation," they condemn a civics book that refers to a future U.S. president as "he or she." Textbooks that mention the shortcomings of George Washington or Thomas Jefferson (including their status as slaveholders) or that seem to make supportive statements of equality between men and women, will not get a Gabler endorsement. They have objected to the use of the word "dang" (implies profanity) and to P.T. Barnum's claim that a sucker is born every minute ("a depressing thought").

Racial issues are particularly important to the Gablers. They oppose mandatory busing to achieve integration, for example, and claim that history textbooks that focus on white racism are themselves racist because they ignore the bigotry of African-Americans. The Gablers rejected one textbook because it claimed that both Martin Luther and Martin Luther King, Jr. were reformers, arguing that, unlike his namesake, Martin Luther was a "religiously-dedicated, non-violent man." The Gablers have also supported other anti-textbook actions in which racism was deeply implicated, such as the Kanawha County protest. (See the Heritage section)

The Gablers argue that the lack of absolutes, even in advanced mathematics, can ruin a student. They have praised a Warsaw, Indiana school board that banned the teaching of calculus and trigonometry. Mel Gabler warned one interviewer, "When a student reads in a math book that there are no absolutes, suddenly every value he's been taught is destroyed. And the next thing you know, the student turns to crime and drugs."

THE INTELLECTUAL RIGHT

The Coors family is a leading supporter of Michigan's Hillsdale College, a little-known, private college already influential in New Right circles. Hillsdale's 150th anniversary capital and endowment campaign, FreedomQuest, seeks to raise $151 million by 1994, in order to raise the school's profile in conservative public policymaking and to establish itself as the academic center of conservative intellectual thought. One Hillsdale brochure noted that a number of the school's outreach efforts, including the Center for Constructive Alternatives (CCA), Shavano Institute for National Leadership, Ludwig von Mises Lecture Series in free market economics, and the monthly journal *Imprimis*, "help generate the ideas and motivation important to Hillsdale's national leadership role."[268]

Hillsdale's Center for Constructive Alternatives and its Shavano Institute for National Leadership sponsor forums on a variety of conservative themes. A September 1989 forum in Detroit, for instance, questioned the desirability of public education. Despite its regular boast that it accepts no federal funds, Hillsdale took State Department money when it had the opportunity to co-sponsor a seminar with the State Department in 1985 on "U.S. and Soviet Values." Jeane Kirkpatrick was the key speaker, appearing with such others as Melvin Lasky, editor of the CIA-funded, London-based *Encounter* magazine.[269] The Shavano Institute received a start-up grant of $50,000 from the Coors Foundation in 1982. Since 1979, the Coors Foundation has donated almost five hundred thousand dollars to Hillsdale College. The Coors corporation has also donated unspecified amounts, and Jeffrey Coors serves as a trustee of the Shavano Institute, as well as of the College.

A list of the school's other supporters reads like a "Who's Who" of the American New Right. The college's promotional videotape, "Ideas Have Consequences," features endorsements from such conservative leaders as Jeane Kirkpatrick, William F. Buckley, and William Simon. Hillsdale's Board of Trustees includes Jeffrey Coors, James Quayle, and Philip Crane, who is also an alumnus. Even Ronald Reagan has praised Hillsdale, commenting that the school's "outreach on national issues enables little Hillsdale to cast such a long shadow."

Although Hillsdale attempts to represent itself as within the conservative mainstream, the school has strong connections to the far right. For example, the college's 1990 book and tape catalog notes that Hillsdale is the repository of the complete Manion Forum collection (of the late John Birch Society National Council member Clarence Manion), representing "the best of American Conservative thought in the post-war era." Audiotapes available from Hillsdale's Manion Forum include "Will They Listen Now?" (Manion's tribute to Joe McCarthy on the first anniversary of his death), as well as tapes by Nicaraguan dictator Somoza, Phyllis Schlafly, and Rhodesian prime minister Ian Smith.

Further, Hillsdale has associated itself with such groups as the World Anti-Communist League (WACL), which works openly with fascist and racist organizations. Hillsdale President George Roche serves on the advisory board of the United States branch of WACL, and an arm of Hillsdale was represented at the 1985 international meeting of WACL in Dallas.[270] Roche is also a member of the far-right Council for National Policy.

Longtime Hillsdale President Roche is opposed in general to social engineering plans, among which he includes affirmative action and public education. Roche has attacked the Civil Rights Restoration Act as "frightening" federal intervention.[271] He calls affirmative action "the putrid backwash of all the tired social engineering schemes" and complains that its advocates are so hypersensitive that a school's unwillingness to set up "advanced bongo drum programs" is called racist.

In his 1977 book, *Education in America*, Roche argues that public education is an immoral appropriation of taxpayer funds. According to Roche, education should be voluntary, and funded, like religion, individually, rather than by the state. Roche asks, "Why should the money of one citizen be taken by force to finance the education of other peoples' children, any more than to finance the building of other peoples' homes?. . . The only lasting solution is to remove education from the hands of the government, restoring responsibility to the student and the parent."[272] Roche's latest book, *One By One: Preserving Values and Freedom in Heartland America*, published in 1990 by the Hillsdale College Press, describes Hillsdale's battle against tomorrow's enemies of the moral order, "the Greens instead of the Reds, the 'New Agers,' the Satanists, ideologues, tax-takers, utopians, self-serving bureaucrats, the immoral and the irresponsible," who always attack "what is normal and morally healthy in favor of things everyone has always regarded as perverse."[273]

The selection of contributors for Hillsdale's monthly magazine, *Imprimis*, also reflects the school's far-right political views. In one issue, Gerda

Bikales, a founder and former executive director of the English Only organization, U.S. English, condemned the advocates of cultural diversity and bilingual education. She attacked the "skilled language planners and other militant advocates" who promote bilingual education, as well as those who "aggressively pursue" diversity and cultural pluralism.[274] Another contributor to Imprimis, Humberto Belli, is a religious cult member whose first anti-Sandinista book was funded by the CIA. Belli also participated in a 1983 Hillsdale forum on Central America with Guatemalan rightist Manuel Ayau. Ayau is a member of Amigos del Pais, a group linked to Guatemalan death squads.[275]

Another Imprimis author, Samuel Blumenfeld, is a longtime John Birch Society activist. Blumenfeld believes that public education is wholly incompatible with American values and calls for an abolition of the public education "monopoly" and a return to "educational freedom." According to Blumenfeld, modern public education fulfills a communist design developed by educational reformer John Dewey in the 1930's.[276] Blumenfeld believes that the groundwork for this design was laid by the utopian movements of the early nineteenth century, which he characterizes as socialists "operating covertly in secret cells in America as early as 1829, before the word socialism was even invented."[277] In his 1981 book Is Public Education Necessary?, Blumenfeld argues that a small group of secular humanists, "more concerned with destroying religion than with freeing man, spearheaded the drive toward public education."[278] Blumenfeld is the author of a number of other books that attack public education, including The NEA: Trojan Horse in American Education, The New Illiterates, The Retreat from Motherhood, and How to Start Your Own Private School—And Why You Need One.

The Heritage Foundation and the Free Congress Foundation have also been noted for their opposition to public education. In their 1988 joint platform, for example, they advocate laws that would allow parents to teach their own children at home rather than send them to school. Although they claim their goal "is to improve public schools, not denigrate them," the platform calls for a concerted attack on public education, saying that critics should emphasize "the failure of the present system" of public education in order to damage "the credibility of the educational establishment." Heritage and the Free Congress Foundation advocate tactics that can split their opposition—the platform calls for education to be "reformed radically."[279]

Accuracy in Academia, a national conservative education watchdog group, has also received extensive Coors support. The group, which was established in 1985 to combat a perceived leftist, Marxist bias on college campuses, asks students to monitor classes and investigates their complaints of biased or inaccurate class presentations. AIA has also distributed such classic attacks on academia as Illiberal Education, Profscam: Professors and the

Demise of Higher Education, The Hollow Men: Politics and Corruption in Higher Education, Poisoned Ivy, and *Academic License.* Accuracy in Academia was founded by Reed Irvine, who also heads AIA's sister group, the twenty-year-old Accuracy in Media, which is funded by Coors as well.

Recently, AIA has played a leading role in the promotion of claims that liberal demands for "political correctness" inhibit academic freedom on campus. Affirmative action programs for racial minorities have been the primary target of this attack. The development of courses in Black, Latin, and Women's Studies have also been condemned by AIA, and the group has been a vocal defender of mandatory coursework in white, Western culture.[280] In 1991, AIA sponsored a Washington, D.C. conference "Politically Incorrect: Fighting the Campus Thought Police," which featured presentations by representatives from other Coors-supported education activists, including the Intercollegiate Studies Institute. Workshop titles included "Affirmative Discrimination on Campus," "Intolerance in the Name of Tolerance," "Marxist Indoctrination in the Academy," and "Fighting Liberal Fascism on Campus."[281]

Accuracy in Academia's publication *Campus Report* is distributed free of charge to college students. Racial issues are particularly important to *Campus Report*. The paper opposes affirmative action programs (as reverse discrimination) and defends courses in Western culture as our "common patrimony."[282] Recent front-page stories have focused on Martin Luther King's alleged plagiarism and Nelson Mandela's ties to communists in South Africa. Other typical articles have praised Grove City College for its eschewal of the Marxist radicalism it sees as rampant on other college campuses and Hillsdale College President George Roche for his college's defense of the free market and traditional values.[283]

Accuracy In Academia played an aggressive role in the defense of J. Philippe Rushton, a psychology professor at the University of Western Ontario who claims that Black people are genetically inferior to whites. AIA Executive Director Leslie Carbone flew to the University to defend Rushton in a speech on campus while AIA's *Campus Report* published a series of articles on the controversy.[284] AIA framed the issues surrounding Rushton's claim as involving academic freedom rather than racism, and AIA quoted with approval defenders of Rushton who deny that his beliefs are racist.

OTHER EDUCATIONAL ENTERPRISES

Coors-supported rightist elements in the education arena that have been previously discussed include Christendom College; Pat Robertson's CBN University (now Regent University), on whose board Holly Coors sits; and the National Association of Christian Educators.[285] Other rightist educational enterprises receiving money from the Coors family include:

■ **Rockford College**, a liberal arts college that teaches and publishes right-wing views, received nearly one-half million dollars from the Coors foundation over the last twelve years. Rockford president Allan Carlson and several college trustees are members of the Council for National Policy. In a well-publicized split in 1989, Rockford Institute ousted Rev. Richard John Neuhaus following his charges that the school was exhibiting signs of xenophobia and an insensitivity to anti-Semitism. Neuhaus wrote in a memo to Carlson that the Institute was maintaining "a running polemic against those whom the reader is invited to view as rootless, deracinated, and cosmopolitan elites," a polemic which amounted, Neuhaus charged, to "the classic language of anti-Semitism."[286] Rockford responded to Neuhaus's complaints by sending five men, including three members of the Board of Directors, to seize Neuhaus's Manhattan office without warning, leaving Neuhaus and several followers on a New York City curb, "surrounded by a few boxes and some garbage bags full of personal stuff."[287]

■ **Hoover Institution**, a research and publishing enterprise that produces studies buttressing Cold War foreign policy themes, has been supported by Coors with sizable grants. Joe Coors served on the Institution's Board of Overseers. Hoover's book publishing arm has also supported the conservative campus newspapers trained and funded by the Institute for Educational Affairs. (*See the Media section*)

■ **Grove College**, which received national attention for its fight against civil rights enforcement, has received Coors funding.

■ **Pepperdine College**, in Malibu, California, has received Coors funding. The very conservative school also hired former Coors aide Jack McCarty (*see the Heritage and Media sections*) as an administrator.

CONCLUSION

The Coors family derives the bulk of its wealth from working- and middle-class people who purchase Coors beer products. The Coors family, through its political operations, then uses its share of the profits from these beer sales to perpetuate and encourage regressive governmental and social policies that serve only the narrow interests of a handful of the very wealthy in our country. That the Coors family is able to cloud this reality is due to the Coors Corporation's high visibility advertising campaign.

The Coors family aids and abets a network of conservative and far-right groups including those which seek to turn back civil rights, destroy trade unions, disregard the fragility of the environment, and promote racial bigotry, homophobia, and male supremacy. The Coors family and their allies also promote a belligerent foreign policy that has claimed lives in Nicaragua, Angola, Mozambique, South Africa, and other countries.

In pursuit of its political agenda, the Coors family network employs or is allied with secretive, authoritarian, and totalitarian political and religious forces which overlap with racist and anti-Semitic elements, all pushing programs which would result in the diminution or dissolution of pluralism and democracy in the United States. Some observers believe that Jeffrey and Peter Coors have moderated the politics of the Coors empire because the Coors Corporation now financially supports some women's, civil rights, and gay and lesbian groups. These donations and advertising dollars represent a pragmatic investment-oriented response to the consumer boycott of Coors products, not a rejection of the bedrock beliefs held by the Coors family.

Through donations to the Coors Political Action Committee, as directors of the family foundation, and with corporate funds, Peter and Jeffrey

Coors continue to fund and support the extreme right. Levels of funding to some rightist groups, such as the Free Congress Foundation, have increased under Jeffrey's leadership. Other, more extreme groups, such as the National Association of Christian Educators, have begun to receive funding only in the past several years. The Coors family's rightist goals are still in place and their influence remains strong. Although the survival and growth of the corporation has required some financial concessions and a shift in public image, the Coors family empire still represents a threat to peace, social justice, pluralism, and democracy.

ENDNOTES

1. This account of the Coors family is based primarily on *Los Angeles Times*, Sept. 18–19, 1988; *Sunday Denver Post*, Sept. 25, 1983, Contemporary magazine; *Denver Business*, May 1987; and *People*, July 7, 1975.

2. Alan Crawford, *Thunder on the Right* (New York: Pantheon, 1980), p. 12.

3. *Washington Post*, May 7, 1975, p. A5; Crawford, pp. 10–12.

4. T. H. Tetens, *The New Germany and the Old Nazis* (New York: Random House, 1961), p. 255, and for related matters, pp. 53, 56–70, 254; *Washington Post*, May 7, 1975, p. A5; *Denver Post*, Sept. 7, 1975, p. 1; author's interview with OUN member.

5. *Boston Globe*, January 16, 1989, p. 10; Chip Berlet, "A Nazi in the Hand is Worth Two in the Bush," *Propaganda Review*, Spring 1989, pp. 26–30; (Oakland) *Tribune*, Dec. 28, 1988, p. A10.

6. *Washington Post*, May 7, 1975, p. A5.

7. For a short profile on Weyrich, see *Washington Post*, March 16, 1989.

8. Paul Weyrich, "Blue Collar or Blue Blood? The New Right Compared with the Old Right," in Robert W. Whitaker, ed., *The New Right Papers* (New York: St. Martin's Press, 1982), p. 52; John Roy Carlson, *Under Cover* (New York: E.P. Dutton, 1943), pp. 54–69; Geoffrey Smith, *To Save a Nation* (New York: Basic Books, 1973), esp. p. 133; Crawford, p. 270.

9. *The New York Times*, Oct. 9, 1975, p. 40.

10. *The New York Times*, Nov. 13, 1975, p. 1; William Rusher, *The Rise of the Right* (New York: William Morrow, 1984), p. 255; CNP membership list.

11. *Washington Post*, May 7, 1975, p. A1; Affidavit of James Lewis, April 22, 1982; *The Charleston Gazette*, November 5, 1974, November 6, 1974, p. 1D, November 10, 1974, December 2, 1974. An unlikely source of support for the Kanawha County protesters came from International Workers Party (IWP) organizers Sema Foxx, Lew Hart, and Nancy Ross. The IWP later evolved into the New

Alliance Party and Nancy Ross currently heads the NAP-spawned Rainbow Lobby in Washington, D.C.

12. *Washington Post*, May 7, 1975, p. A1.

13. C. H. Simonds, "The Strange Case of Willis Carto," *National Review*, Sept. 10, 1971, pp. 978–989; *Wall Street Journal*, Sept. 28, 1984, p. 46; *Searchlight*, June 1984, p. 9; *Searchlight*, Sept. 1984, p. 2.

14. Roger Pearson, *Race and Civilization* (London: Clair Press, 1966), title page; Roger Pearson, *Eugenics and Race* (London: Clair Press, 1966), p. 26; Robert Wistrich, *Who's Who in Nazi Germany* (New York: Macmillan, 1982), pp. 114–115; *Right*, June 1959, p. 1. *Right* was Willis Carto's newsletter which endorsed, for example, the American Nazi Party.

15. *Washington Post*, May 28, 1978, p. C1; Scott Anderson and Jon Lee Anderson, *Inside the League* (New York: Dodd, Mead, 1986).

16. Edwin J. Feulner, ed., *China—The Turning Point* (Washington, D.C.: Council on American Affairs, 1976).

17. *Wall Street Journal*, Sept. 28, 1984, p. 46; Ernest van den Haag, "Intelligence or Prejudice?" *National Review*, Dec. 1, 1964, pp. 1059–63; *Washington Post*, May 21, 1964, p. A8; *Policy Review*, Summer 1989, masthead; *The Journal of Social, Political and Economic Studies*, Fall, 1984, masthead; Coors Foundation, IRS Form 990–PF, 1978, 1979.

18. *Washington Post*, May 7, 1975, p. A1.

19. *China: The Turning Point; Wall Street Journal*, Sept. 28, 1984, p. 46.

20. U.S. House, Committee on International Relations, Subcommittee on International Organizations, *Investigation of Korean-American Relations*, 95th Cong., 2nd Sess., Oct. 31, 1978, pp. 106, 312, 317, 319, 369.

21. *The Nation*, Jan. 23, 1989; *In These Times*, Jan. 11–17, 1989, p. 4; Heritage Foundation 1985: List of Major Corporate Sponsors.

22. Heritage Publications Catalog, 1986; *In These Times*, Jan. 11–17, 1989, p. 4.

23. *Investigation of Korean-American Relations*, pp. 317–318, 321, 329, 331; *Mother Jones*, May 1981, p. 12; Michael Warder, "Bribemasters," *Chronicles*, June 1988, p. 31; *Extra!* Sept./Oct. 1988, p. 6.

24. *Kansas City Star*, Dec. 20, 1987; *Mother Jones*, May 1981, p. 12; *Seattle Times*, Feb. 12, 1989, p. 1; *Washington Herald*, Feb. 8–21, 1988, p. 12; author's visit to Heritage building.

25. *Washington Post*, June 29, 1989; U.S. House, *Investigation of Korean-American Relations*, p. 24.

26. Charles Heatherly, ed., *Mandate for Leadership* (Washington, D.C.: Heritage Foundation, 1981).

27. *Oklahoma Times*, March 25, 1981.

28. *Denver Post*, Jan. 20, 1982.

29. *Atlantic Monthly*, Jan. 1986, pp. 78–79.

30. Stuart M. Butler, Michael J. Sanera and W. Bruce Weinrod, *Mandate for Leadership II* (Washington, D.C.: Heritage Foundation, 1984).

31. *The New York Times*, Nov. 17, 1985, p. 31; *Boston Herald*, March 19, 1985; *Denver Post*, Nov. 23, 1984, p. 3A.

32. *The New York Times*, Aug. 8, 1984, p. 12; *Mandate for Leadership II*; Coors Foundation, IRS 990–PF, 1977, 1985.

33. *The New York Times*, Nov. 20, 1984; *Denver Post*, Dec. 5, 1984; *Mandate for Leadership II*, pp. 264–270; Coors Foundation, IRS 990–PF, 1977, 1985.

34. *The New York Times*, Nov. 17, 1985, p. 31.

35. *Atlantic Monthly*, Jan. 1986, p. 69.

36. Crawford, p. 278; *Washington Post*, May 6, 1975, p. 1.

37. Crawford, p. 278.

38. *Columbia Journalism Review*, March/April, 1975, p. 19; Crawford, p. 10.

39. Thomas McIntyre, *The Fear Brokers* (Boston: Beacon Press, 1979), p. 68.

40. *Ibid.*, p. 69.

41. Crawford, p. 55.

42. *Washington Post*, Aug. 29, 1976, p. 3; Crawford, pp. 236–37.

43. Crawford, p. 237.

44. *Human Events*, Sept. 11, 1976, pp. 3–4.

45. McIntyre, p. 70; CSFC Federal Election Commission records, 1977–78 election cycle.

46. Sara Diamond, *Spiritual Warfare: The Politics of the Christian Right* (Boston: South End Press, 1989), p. 60.

47. Crawford, p. 162; CSFC FEC records, 1979–80 election cycle.

48. Conference Programs for Allies for Renewal, a Word of God front activity, 1980's; for a general discussion of Word of God, see author's articles in *National Catholic Reporter*, Nov. 18, 1988, p. 5.

49. Author's interviews with former members.

50. Allies for Renewal Conference Program, June 1989.

51. Diamond, pp. 128–30.

52. WOG minutes, 1974; Diamond, pp. 62, 70, 78–79, 127, 254 (fn 118).

53. Diamond, p. 130.

54. Anatole Fellowship letter, Santa Rosa, California, signed by Mike Kusten, n.d.

55. *Anatole Alert*, n.d.; Diamond, pp. 179–80.

56. National Pro-Family Coalition, *Action!* Feb. 1986; *Detroit Free Press*, June 8, 1986, p. 15A.

57. NACE letter, June 1989; Coors Foundation, IRS 990–PF, 1986, 1987, 1988.

58. COR letterhead, April 1989.

59. Thomas Case, "TFP: Catholic or Cult?" *Fidelity*, May 1989, pp. 22–29; *Fidelity*, Sept. 1989, pp. 2–10; *Family, Law and Democracy Report*, March 1989, pp. 10–11.

60. Program of the First Annual Conservative Leadership Conference, December 1989.

61. FCF Annual Report, 1988, pp. 22–23.

62. *Ibid.*, p. 22.

63. *Ibid.*, pp. 22–23.

64. *Ibid*, p. 22; *Legatus*, Sept. 1987, p. 1 (where Monaghan is described as the founder and a new *Legatus* coordinator is described as a previous employee of Servant Ministries, a branch of the Word of God network); *Legatus*, April 1988, p. 5.

65. FCF Annual Report, 1986, p. 33.

66. FCF Annual Report, 1988, p. 24; *New Republic*, Dec. 23, 1985, p.11; *The New York Times*, May 29, 1984; *The New York Times*, April 25, 1989.

67. FCF Annual Report, 1988, p. 25.

68. *Freedom Fighter*, Jan. 1989, p. 2.

69. *Ibid*; author's attendance at WACL conference, San Diego, California, Sept. 1984.

70. *The New York Times*, March 24, 1988; *New York Times*, May 19, 1987, p. A35; *In These Times*, Aug. 31–Sept. 6, 1988, p. 2. See also William Minter, "The Mozambican National Resistance (Renamo) as Described by Ex-participants, Research Report Submitted to: Ford Foundation and Swedish International Development Agency," Washington, D.C. 1989. See also the film, "Mozambique: Riding Out the Storm," Prod. by Alter-Cine, Dir. by Bill Turnley and Ole Gjerstad, 1989 (Available from California Newsreel, 949 9th St., Rm. 420, San Francisco, CA, 94103).

71. *Washington Times*, Jan. 19, 1989, p. H-5; *Freedom Fighter*, Jan. 1989.

72. Telephone interview with Mike Lythgoe, Vice President for Development and College Relations, Christendom College, Aug. 9, 1989; FCF Annual Report, 1986, p. 34; FCF Annual Report, 1988; Adolph Coors Foundation Annual Report, 1988, p. 10; Coors Foundation, IRS 990–PF; *Afghan Update*, Sept. 16, 1985, p. 6. See also *Covert Action Information Bulletin*, #26, p. 3 for detailed information on Vernon Walters.

73. Compare FCF Annual Report, 1988 with CNP Quarterly Membership Meeting Program, Orlando, Florida, Feb. 3–4, 1989.

74. *Intercessors for America Newsletter*, Sept. 1986; *Intercessors for America Newsletter*, Jan. 1989, p. 1; *Mother Jones*, Feb./March 1981; COR letterhead, April 1989; Adolph Coors Foundation Annual Report, 1988; CNP Executive Committee Meeting, Baltimore, Maryland, May 12, 1989.

75. *Intercessors for America Newsletter*, Jan. 1989, p. 4; FCF Annual Report, 1988; Crawford, p. 161.

76. CNP Executive Committee Meeting, Baltimore, Maryland, May 12, 1989.

77. Heritage Foundation Annual Report, 1988; Rockford Institute Annual Report, 1983.

78. *Detroit Free Press*, May 18, 1989, p. 1; *Mother Jones*, Feb./March 1981, p. 34; Conservative Caucus letterhead, June 1989.

79. CNP Board of Governors Meeting, List of Member-Participants, Dallas, Texas, Aug. 17–18, 1984.

80. FCF Annual Report, 1988.

81. *The New York Times*, June 15, 1984; *In These Times*, April 8–14, 1987.

82. Anderson and Anderson, pp. 256–57, 270; Author's attendance at WACL meetings.

83. Free Congress Research and Education Foundation Memorandum, by Charles Moser, Sept. 24, 1982.

84. *Ukrainian Quarterly*, Summer 1984, masthead; John Armstrong, *Ukrainian Nationalism*, 2nd ed. (New York and London: Columbia University Press, 1963); Phillip Friedman, *Roads to Extinction: Essays on the Holocaust* (Philadelphia: Jewish Publication Society of America, and New York: Conference on Jewish Social Studies, 1980); Joe Conason, "Reagan and the War Crimes Lobby," *Village Voice*, May 14, 1985; Lubomyr R. Wynar, *Encyclopedic Directory of Ethnic Organizations in the United States* (Littleton, Colorado: Libraries Unlimited, 1975), p. 150; Alexander Dallin, *German Rule in Russia, 1941–45: A Study in Occupation Policies* (New York: St. Martin's Press, 1957). For UCCA's orientation, see, for example, two articles which praise the Waffen SS: Edward M. O'Connor, "Our Open Society Under Attack By the Despotic State," *Ukrainian Quarterly*, Spring 1984, pp. 17–49, esp. pp. 48–49; and Wasyl Veryha, "General Pavlo Shandruk," *Ukrainian Quarterly*, Summer 1984, pp. 164–177. For a discussion of fascists recruited by U.S. intelligence, see Christopher Simpson, *Blowback: America's Recruitment of Nazis and its Effects on the Cold War* (New York: Weidenfeld & Nicholson, 1988).

85. "UCCA Calls for Congressional Hearings into OSI," *Ukrainian Review*, Summer 1985, p. 96.

86. Coalitions for America letter, April 18, 1985.

87. (Pittsburgh, PA) *Post-Gazette*, Sept. 16, 1988; telephone interview with Laszlo Pasztor, January 24, 1990. Interview conducted by Chip Berlet with Pasztor at his FCF building office in Washington, D.C. In the *Post-Gazette* article, Pasztor was reported as currently a "volunteer" at the Free Congress Research and Education Foundation; however Pasztor is supplied with an internal telephone number at FCF (listed as extension 48 as of January 21, 1990) and calls to the FCF main number are routinely connected through to Pasztor. Pasztor confirms that for several years he has generally worked in the FCF office complex Tuesday afternoons through Fridays.

88. Randolph L. Braham, "Boring From Within: The Case of Laszlo Pasztor," *Midstream: A Jewish Review*, June/July 1989, pp. 25–28. Prof. Braham is Director of the Csengeri Institute for Holocaust Studies at the City University of

New York Graduate Center and author of the definitive two-volume study *The Politics of Genocide: The Holocaust in Hungary* (New York: Columbia University Press, 1981). Prof. Braham has also supplied and translated copies of official Hungarian court documents dated 1945 to 1949 regarding Pasztor's conviction for collaboration. The documents provided by Braham confirm the arrest of Pasztor on December 5, 1945, articulate a specific list of charges for which Pasztor was convicted on March 14, 1946 after an open trial. Pasztor was then sentenced to five years in jail. The documents show that in 1948 the conviction was appealed, and in 1949 the appeals court reaffirmed Pasztor's Arrow Cross membership and Nazi collaboration but effectively reduced his sentence to time served, whereupon he was released from jail. For background on the Arrow Cross and general time frame in Hungary, see also Nora Levin, *The Holocaust: The Destruction of European Jewry 1933–1945* (New York: T.Y. Crowell, 1968; Schocken Books, 1973), pp. 610–11, 644, 653–55, 662–64.

89. Interview with Pasztor, Jan. 24, 1990; Chip Berlet and Holly Sklar, "Harbinger of Democracy? The N.E.D.'s Ex-Nazi Adviser," *The Nation*, April 2, 1990, pp. 450–451.

90. *Washington Post*, Nov. 21, 1971, p. A1; Simpson, p. 273; Author's interview with Laszlo Pasztor, Washington, D.C., May 15, 1985.

91. Coalitions for America brochure, n.d., obtained in 1989; Free Congress Research and Education Foundation, Annual Report, 1986; Interview with Pasztor, Jan. 24, 1990.

92. Interview with Laszlo Pasztor, Jan. 24, 1990; telephone interview with White House Scheduling Office, Washington, D.C., January 26, 1990 (conducted by Chip Berlet). A source close to FCF confirmed the details of the White House meeting.

93. Interview with Pasztor, Jan. 24, 1990; Berlet and Sklar, *The Nation*, April 2, 1990, pp. 450–451.

94. *ABN Correspondence*, May–June 1989, pp. 14, 49; Simpson, pp. 269–73.

95. Interview with Pasztor, Jan. 24, 1990; Minutes, National Endowment for Democracy, March 17, 1989, pp. 17, 21.

96. *Newsweek*, Jan. 29, 1990, p. 48.

97. FCF Annual Report, 1989; Adolph Coors Foundation Annual Report, 1988; Coors Foundation, FEC Records, 1977–1988.

98. Rodney Clapp, "Democracy as Heresy," *Christianity Today*, Feb. 20, 1987, p. 17.

99. Greg Garland, "North was a member of a private group once based in Baton Rouge," (Baton Rouge) *State Times*, Jan. 8, 1987, p. 1A; CNP Board of Governors Meeting, List of Member Participants, Dallas, Texas, Aug. 17–18, 1984; Executive Committee Meeting, CNP, Baltimore, Maryland, May 12, 1989.

100. Author's contact with a source close to CNP.

101. Board of Governors Meeting, List of Member Participants, Dallas, Texas, Aug. 17–18, 1984; Author's contact with a source close to CNP.

102. Davis gained national headlines during this period because he had just been acquitted of charges of murdering his stepdaughter and masterminding a murder-for-hire scheme.

103. Greg Garland, "Conservative Council for National Policy got off to an unlikely start," (Baton Rouge) *State Times*, Jan. 8, 1987, p. 1A. *Newsweek*, July 6, 1981, pp. 48–49, quotes LaHaye, "We must remove all humanists from public office and replace them with pro-moral political leaders." In his newsletter, *Capitol Report*, July 1989, p. 1, LaHaye reiterated this view.

104. CNP Board of Governors Confidential Mailing List, Baton Rouge, 1984, for use until Jan. 1, 1985; CIS letterhead, May 1989; Inter-American Security Educational Institute Speakers Bureau, n.d.

105. *Newsweek*, July 6, 1981, p. 49; (Baton Rouge) *State Times*, Jan. 8, 1987, p. 1A.

106. Author's confidential interview, CNP member.

107. Greg Garland, "North was member of private group," *State Times*, Jan. 9, 1987, p. 1A; U.S., S. Rept. No. 100–216 and H. Rept. No. 100–433, *Report of the Congressional Committees Investigating the Iran Contra Affair with Supplemental, Minority and Additional Views*, 100th Cong., 1st Sess. (Washington: GPO, 1987), p. 97.

108. CNP Quarterly Membership Meeting Program, Orlando, Florida, Feb. 3–4, 1989; Thomas B. Edsall and David Vise, "CBS Fight a Litmus Test for Conservatives," *Washington Post*, March 31, 1985, p. A1; Thomas B. Edsall and David Vise, "Battle for CBS Takes On Air of Mudslinging Contest," *Washington Post*, March 31, 1985, p. A16.

109. *The New York Times*, Dec. 11, 1977, p. 76; (Louisville, KY) *Courier-Journal*, Oct. 16, 1977; Pioneer Fund, IRS 990–PF, 1976; Roger Pearson, *Eugenics and Race* (London: Clair Press, 1966), p. 26; CNP Quarterly Membership Meeting Program, Orlando, Florida, Feb. 3–4, 1989; *The Five Minute Report (For and about the members of the Council for National Policy)*, May 26, 1989.

110. All members of the CNP listed here appear on the Board of Governors Confidential Mailing List, Baton Rouge, 1984; CNP Quarterly Membership Meeting Program, Orlando, Florida, Feb. 3–4, 1989.

111. *Charlotte Observer*, March 9, 1986; *Indianapolis Star*, March 30, 1973, p. 1. The film, *High Frontier*, produced by the organization High Frontier, credits Lincoln Log Homes with providing financial support for the film. The religious cult, Church Universal and Triumphant (CUT), is discussed in the *Los Angeles Times*, Feb. 11, 1980, pt. 2, p. 1. In 1988, Gene Vosseler, chairman of CUT Department of Theology, made a nation-wide tour on behalf of High Frontier, according to the *High Frontier Newswatch*, April 1988, p. 8 and *Los Angeles Times*, April 2, 1980, pt. 2, p. 5. The AIDS fundraising scheme was revealed in the *Chicago Sun-Times*, Jan. 21, 1990, p. 22.

112. Telephone interview with a spokesperson, Public Records, Department of Justice, Aug. 8, 1989.

113. *The New York Times*, March 23, 1988.

114. *National Reporter*, Winter 1985, p. 19. McGoff was investigated briefly by the

Justice Department for allegedly acting as an unregistered agent of the South African regime, but no charges were filed.

115. *New American*, July 3, 1989, list of contributing editors; *The Nation*, Sept. 26, 1988. See also McAlvany's letter and *The Nation*'s reply on Nov. 14, 1988. McAlvany said about Tutu, "The least you can do is remove the idiot's passport and not let him travel over to our country, and somebody might want to even shoot him—I repeal that. I don't say shoot him . . . Somebody ought to do something to make him stop what he's doing." McAlvany said in his letter of complaint that *The Nation* had "attributed to me a most damaging and inaccurate statement, one that does not reflect either my actual views or my complete remarks on the occasion cited."

116. Pearson's *Journal of Social, Political and Economic Studies*, Editorial Board Advisory Committee list, Fall 1983, Fall 1984.

117. John S. Saloma, *Ominous Politics: The New Conservative Labyrinth* (New York: Hill and Wang/Farrar, Strauss and Giroux, 1984), pp. 15–16; *The New York Times*, Nov. 13, 1975, p. 1.

118. Gary K. Clabaugh, *Thunder on the Right: The Protestant Fundamentalists* (Chicago: Nelson-Hall Co., 1974), pp. 47, 102, 127; *Group Research Report*, July 30, 1963, pp. 55–56; Group Research Special Report on Dr. Billy James Hargis, Oct. 10, 1962.

119. Lucy Dawidowicz, *Commentary*, Dec. 1980; CNP Biographical Statement Memo; Wynar, p. 150; Ralph Scott, "The Bookshelf: *The Dispossessed Majority*," *Voice of Americans of German Descent*, Oct. 1975, p. 4; Barry Mehler, *The Nation*, May 7, 1988, p. 641; *Des Moines Register*, July 13, 1988, p. 4A; *The New York Times*, Dec. 11, 1977, p. 76; *Washington Post*, March 31, 1985, pp. A1, A16; Pioneer Fund, Inc., Federal Income Tax Return, Form 990-PF, 1976.

120. *Wall Street Journal*, Aug. 16, 1985, p. 1.

121. *Christianity Today*, Feb. 20, 1987, p. 17; FCF Institute for Government and Politics, Conference on Criminal Justice Reform Program, Arlington, Virginia, Sept. 27, 1983.

122. Gary North, *Backward, Christian Soldiers* (Tyler, Texas: Institute for Christian Economics, 1984), p. 13.

123. *Christianity Today*, Feb. 20, 1987, p. 17.

124. Diamond, p. 78.

125. *Washington Times*, Dec. 7, 1987, p. 5.

126. McIntyre, p. 92; Adolph Coors Company Charitable Contribution Recipients, 1985.

127. *Wall Street Journal*, Aug. 16, 1985, p. 1; *The Right Report*, Nov. 19, 1976, pp. 1–3; *The Right Report*, Dec. 17, 1976; *The Right Report*, May 6, 1977; *Human Events*, Sept. 11, 1976, p. 3; CNP Board of Governors Meeting, List of Member Participants, Dallas, Texas, Aug. 17–18, 1984.

128. *Boston Globe*, Sept. 14, 1988; *Freedom Writer*, Vol. 6, No. 3; *Manhattan Inc.*, July 1989; COR letterhead, April 1989.

129. Phyllis Schlafly, *A Choice Not an Echo*, 3rd ed. (Alton, Illinois: Pere Marquette Press, 1964), pp. 6, 25–26, 112–113.

130. George Seldes, *Witness to a Century* (New York: Ballantine Books, 1987); Chip Berlet, "Cardinal Mindszenty: Heroic Anti-Communist or Anti-Semite or Both?" *St. Louis Journalism Review*, April 1988.

131. "O'Duffys Irish Legion: Blue Shirts and Shamrocks in Spain's Civil War," *Soldier of Fortune*, March 1985, p. 74; *Soldier of Fortune*, Aug. 1984, pp. 50–52; CNP Board of Governors Meeting, List of Member Participants, Dallas, Texas, Aug. 17–18, 1984; Brown, who has made donations of at least one hundred dollars for four of the last five years would automatically be considered an associate member of CNP.

132. Gary Allen, *None Dare Call it Conspiracy* (Seal Beach, California: Concord Press, 1971), pp. 87, 98, 105; American Opinion Wholesale Book Division Order Form, March 1972.

133. *New American*, Dec. 5, 1988, p. 60; J. Allen Broyles, *The John Birch Society: Anatomy of a Protest* (Boston: Beacon, 1964, 1966); Arnold Forster and Benjamin Epstein, *The Radical Right: Report on the John Birch Society and its Allies* (New York: Vintage, 1967); Daniel Bell, ed., *The Radical Right* (Garden City, New York: Anchor/Doubleday, 1955, 1971).

134. *Washington Post*, May 4, 1975, p. A4.

135. Crawford, p. 96.

136. Harry Hurt, *Texas Rich* (New York: Norton, 1981), p. 369; CNP Board of Governors Meeting, Dallas, Texas, Aug. 17–18, 1984; CNP Executive Committee Meeting, Baltimore, Maryland, May 12, 1989. For connections between CNP and Western Goals, compare CNP Board of Governors list with *Western Goals Report*, Spring 1984, p. ii, listing Western Goals Advisory Board members.

137. CNP Executive Committee Meeting, Baltimore, Maryland, May 12, 1989, election of new members.

138. *Ibid*.

139. Adolph Coors Foundation Annual Reports, 1985 to 1988; Coors Foundation, IRS 990–PF, 1985, 1986, 1987.

140. William Casey, former CIA Director, participated in discussions within an American Bar Association committee which led to the creation of NSIC, and Casey eventually was involved with NSIC for several years until he resigned to accept a federal appointment from President Nixon. The NSIC spokesperson argues that Casey was not *officially* a founder or founding director of the NSIC, although several published articles call Casey an NSIC founder. Nevertheless, Casey's seminal role in forming the NSIC is easily demonstrated and reluctantly acknowledged.

141. Frank Barnett, "A Proposal for Political Warfare," *Military Review*, March 1961, p. 3; Roy Godson, *Intelligence Requirements for the 1980's: Covert Action* (Washington, D.C., New Brunswick, New Jersey and London: NSIC and Transaction Books, 1981).

142. Barnett, Tovar and Shultz, *Special Operations and U.S. Strategy* consists of the proceedings of this conference.

143. *Ibid.*, p. 301.

144. A nine-volume series, *Intelligence Requirements for the 1980's* is published by NSIC and was distributed by Transaction Books, New Brunswick, New Jersey and London, and later by Lexington Books, Lexington, Massachusetts. The entire series is available from NSIC, 1730 Rhode Island Avenue, N.W., Washington, D.C. 20036.

145. *Ibid.*; Coalitions for America brochure, n.d., received 1989, p. 7.

146. ASCF letterhead, July 1986; Coors Foundation, IRS 990–PF, 1977, 1980.

147. Frank Donner, *Age of Surveillance* (New York: Vintage/Random House, 1980), p. 423; *Newsweek*, July 27, 1970, p. 20; William Turner, *Power on the Right* (Berkeley, California: Ramparts Press, 1971), pp. 199–200; *The New York Times*, July 10, 1958, p. 56.

148. *Journal of International Relations*, Winter 1977, title page. The contention that ASC's Coalition for Peace Through Strength contains many groups with fascist, racist, and anti- Semitic backgrounds has been documented at length in the author's *Old Nazis, the New Right and the Republican Party* (Boston, Massachusetts: South End Press, 1988, 1991), see especially footnotes 122–145, 256–298. The author began by examining the ASC's Coalition for Peace Through Strength and found an overlap with the Republican Heritage Groups Council. The footnotes cited above refer back to primary sources explaining the history and nature of the individual groups.

149. *Detroit News*, July 1, 1989, p. 12B; The Military and Hospitaller Order of Saint Lazarus of Jerusalem Member Directory, 1983.

150. *A Strategy for Peace Through Strength* (Boston, Virginia: ASCF, 1984); Australia, *Commonwealth-New South Wales Joint Task Force on Drug Trafficking: Report of Royal Commission*, Vol. 2, Nugan Hand (part 1), June 1982, pp. 298–299, 303–304; *Wall Street Journal*, Aug. 24, 25, 26, 1982; Anderson and Anderson, pp. 55–56.

151. Telephone interview with Faye McAteer at Religious Roundtable, Memphis, Tennessee, Aug. 9, 1989.

152. *Saturday Evening Post*, April 1985, pp. 58, 62; Diamond, p. 251, fn. 42; COR letterhead April 1989; *Rocky Mountain News*, Feb. 21, 1986, p. 6.

153. *Sojourners*, April 1986, pp. 10–11.

154. U.S., House, Committee on Foreign Affairs, Staff Report, *State Department and Intelligence Community Involvement in Domestic Activities Related to the Iran/ Contra Affair*, Sept. 7, 1988, pp. 26–27; *Village Voice*, Oct. 13, 1987; Adolph Coors Foundation Annual Report, 1988.

155. TCC letterhead, Advisory Board, April 1988; TCC Citizens' Cabinet Press Release, May 18, 1977, lists Joe Coors as a member of the Organizing Committee. For funding, see TCC Research and Education, Inc., 1986 financial statement, which lists a $10,000 grant from Coors in 1986; the statement also lists $5,000 donations each from Bo Hi Pak, Robert Krieble, and Richard Shoff, which were collected at a TCC-sponsored Jonas Savimbi fundraising dinner.

156. TCC Citizens' Cabinet Press Release, May 18, 1977; *American Opinion*, Jan. 1963, masthead; Crawford, p. 97; *Chicago Tribune*, June 22, 1986, p. 14; *The New York Times Magazine*, Nov. 23, 1986, p. 63; Leonard Zeskind, *It's Not Populism—America's New Populist Party: A Fraud by Racists and Anti-Semites* (Atlanta, Georgia: Center for Democratic Renewal, 1984); Chip Berlet, "Trashing the Birchers: Secrets of the Paranoid Right," *Boston Phoenix*, July 14–20, 1989, p. 10; Chip Berlet and Russ Bellant, "Radio's Not Pizza: Valerio's right-wing ties," *Boston Phoenix*, Sept. 8–14, 1989, p. 8.

157. *Howard Phillips' Issues and Strategy Bulletin*, April 3, 1989; *McAlvany Intelligence Advisor*, Fall 1988, p. 1; *McAlvany Intelligence Advisor*, March 1989, p. 1; "South Africa 1987: Twelfth Annual Financial Geopolitical Tour," Conservative Caucus direct mailing, n.d.; *Grassroots*, the newsletter of the Conservative Caucus, Aug. 1985; and *New American*, Jan. 27, 1986, p. 32.

158. "Dear Fellow-Traveler" letter, Nov. 30, 1988, p. 7; *Washington Times*, Jan. 19, 1989, p. H5; *The Windhoek Advertiser*, Dec. 15, 1988, p. 1; letter from Howard Phillips to Assistant Secretary of State for African Affairs, March 16, 1989.

159. *Indianapolis Star*, March 30, 1973, p. 1; *Charlotte Observer*, March 9, 1986, p. 1.

160. *Washington Post*, March 31, 1985; CNP Board of Governors List, Dallas, Texas, Aug. 17–18, 1984; Barry Mehler, "The New Eugenics: Academic Racism in the U.S. Today," *Israel Horizons*, Jan./Feb. 1984, pp. 25–27.

161. Conservative Caucus letterhead; *Charlotte Observer*, March 9, 1986.

162. *Los Angeles Times*, Sept. 19, 1988, pt. 1, pp. 17, 18.

163. Coors Boycott Factsheet, Massachusetts AFL-CIO, n.d.

164. "The ERA-Gay-AIDS Connection" brochure, Alton, Illinois, Eagle Forum, n.d; "On Sept. 22, 1983, the U.S. House Passed the Hyde Amendment" brochure, Alton, Illinois, Eagle Forum, n.d; Sasha Gregory-Lewis, "Danger on the Right: Stop-ERA: A Choice or An Echo? (Part II: Mega-Bucks to Mobilize Footsoldiers)," *The Advocate*, Nov. 16, 1977.

165. Tim LaHaye, fundraising letters, Jan. and Aug. 1989; Tim LaHaye, "The ACLU: One of the Most Harmful Organizations in America," *Capital Report* (Special Edition), [1988]; Tim LaHaye, *The Unhappy Gays: What Everyone Should Know About Homosexuality* (Wheaton, Illinois: Tyndale House, 1978). In *The Unhappy Gays*, LaHaye asserts that the Antichrist himself may be a homosexual.

166. *The New York Times*, Dec. 27, 1987; *San Francisco Chronicle & Examiner*, Sept. 7, 1986.

167. *Ibid.; The New Republic*, March 28, 1988, pp. 18–19; *Boston Globe*, Nov. 16, 1987, p. 1.

168. *Inquiry*, August 1981, pp. 13–18; "ERA Rears Its Ugly Head Again" fundraising letter, March 8, 1983.

169. *Denver Post*, Dec. 24, 1981, p. 3A; Advisory Committee of the Editorial Board, *Journal for Social, Political and Economic Affairs*, Fall 1984, masthead.

170. Mark B. Liedl, ed., *Issues '88: A Platform for America; Volume I: Domestic Policy Planks* (Washington, D.C.: Free Congress Research and Education Foundation, 1988), pp. v–vi; Couple to Couple League International, Inc. fundraising letter, Autumn 1989, masthead.

171. *Issues '88: Domestic Policy Planks*, pp. 26–27.

172. *Ibid.*, pp. 50, 106.

173. *Ibid.*, pp. 24, 44, 59–60; *Issues '88: Volume I—Domestic Policy Planks*, pp. 59–61, 215–16, 226–27.

174. *Issues '88: Social Policy Planks*, pp. 54–57, 64–67.

175. *Issues '88: Social Policy Planks*, pp. 23–41; *Issues '88: Domestic Policy Planks*, pp. 60–67.

176. *Issues '88: Social Policy Planks*, pp. 36, 62–64, 87–89, 107–108, 131.

177. *Los Angeles Times*, Sept. 19, 1988, p. 1.

178. Enrique Rueda, *Gays, AIDS and You* (Old Greenwich, Connecticut: Devin Adair, 1987), p. vii.

179. *Ibid.*, pp. vii, 9, 40, 65.

180. *Issues '88: Social Policy Planks*, pp. 59–61.

181. *Gay Community News*, Nov. 30, 1985, p. 3.; "Coors Banned in Boston," Boston City Council Press Release, Jan. 16, 1986; *Gay Community News*, Letter to the Editor, Jan. 11, 1986, p. 4.

182. *Los Angeles Times*, Sept. 18, 1988, p. 30.

183. *Time*, Dec. 26, 1977. See also, for example, Sworn Statement of Richard Anderson, Sept. 28, 1977; Sworn Statement of John Kincannon, Sept. 20, 1977.

184. *Washington Post*, Oct. 1, 1975.

185. *Denver Post*, Aug. 26, 1970, p. 5.

186. *Ibid.*, p. 5.

187. *Rocky Mountain News*, Feb. 24, 1984, p. 64; Transcript of Coors' speech, p. 5. Succeeding quotes are also from this transcript. In *Rocky Mountain News*, Aug. 26, 1987 and *Denver Post*, Aug. 26, 1987, there is a discussion of the resolution of a lawsuit filed by Coors against *Rocky Mountain News* as a result of this incident.

188. "The Black Community Responds to Bill Coors," an undated political flyer signed by a number of community members.

189. *Christian Science Monitor*, March 31, 1989, p. 1.

190. Richard N. Holwill, ed., *Agenda '83* (Washington, D.C.: Heritage Foundation, 1983), p. 207.

191. *Mandate for Leadership*, pp. 448–49.

192. Mark Bohannon, Mary Buckler and David Osborne, "Major Right Wing Organizations," prepared by NEA Teacher Rights, n.d.; *The New Right in the States: The Groups, The Issues and the Strategies* (Washington, D.C.: Conference on Alternative State and Local Policies, n.d.).

193. *Washington Post*, Aug. 21, 1985, p. B1; *Group Research Report*, April 1984, p. 14; Coalition for Religious Freedom brochure, n.d.

194. Paul Weyrich, "Blue Collar or Blue Blood? The New Right Compared with the Old Right," in Robert Whitaker, ed., *The New Right Papers* (New York: St. Martin's Press, 1982), p. 53; Robert Hoy, "Lid on a Boiling Pot," in *The New Right Papers*, pp. 90–91.

195. Robert Hoy, "Lid on a Boiling Pot," in *The New Right Papers*, p. 103; Crawford, pp. 307–308; *Spotlight*, Jan. 20, 1986, p. 17; *Spotlight*, June 2, 1986, p. 15.

196. Interview with Paul Fromm, Aug. 20, 1989. See also Julian Sher, *White Hoods: Canada's Ku Klux Klan* (Vancouver: New Star Books, 1983), p. 78; *Toronto Star*, Oct. 8, 1983, p. B8.

197. *Wall Street Journal*, Sept. 6, 1984, p. 1; FCF Criminal Justice Reform Conference brochure, 1983; Adolph Coors Foundation Annual Report, 1984, p. 16.

198. Coors Foundation Annual Report, Form 990, 1981.

199. Interviews with local Chicano activists; League of United Latin American Citizens (LULAC) letter, Feb. 5, 1984, from state LULAC president Angie Camacho to National LULAC president Mario Obledo.

200. *Ibid.*

201. Interviews with Denver-area Chicano activists.

202. *Hispanic Business*, Sept. 1987, p. 14; *Rocky Mountain News*, Sept. 18, 1986; *Los Angeles Times*, Nov. 13, 1984, p. 29.

203. *Los Angeles Times*, Oct. 20, 1988; interview with Rita Montero.

204. The North-South Institute brochure, n.d.

205. *Rocky Mountain News*, Sept. 23, 1988, p. 16.

206. Independence Institute letterhead, 1988; Coors Foundation Annual Report, 1988.

207. *Chicago Tribune*, Aug. 10, 1986; R.E. "Rusty" Butler, Ph.D., *On Creating a Hispanic America: A Nation Within a Nation?* (Washington, D.C.: Council for Inter-American Security, 1985), p. 9.

208. The North-South Institute brochure, n.d.

209. U.S. Border Control letter, n.d.; Council for Inter-American Security brochure, n.d.; Gun Owners of America document, Nov. 26, 1986; FCF Annual Report, 1986, p. 39; Coors Foundation Annual Report, 1982, 1985, 1986.

210. *Los Angeles Times*, Nov. 13, 1984; *Los Angeles Times*, Oct. 20, 1988; *Arizona Republic*, Oct. 30, 1988, p. C1; *Arizona Republic*, Nov. 16, 1988; *Denver Post*, Oct. 18, 1988, p. 1A.

211. Anderson and Anderson, pp. 150–52; author's attendance at WACL conventions, 1984 and 1985.

212. *Washington Post*, May 3, 1985; *Westword*, May 29–June 4, 1985.

213. Anderson and Anderson, p. 223–24; Christopher Dickey, *With the Contras* (New York: Simon and Schuster, 1985), pp. 82–84, 92, 95–96, 113, 117, 119, 179; *Covert Action Information Bulletin*, Winter 1986, pp. 15–20.

214. Tom Barry, Deb Preusch and Beth Sims, *The New Right Humanitarians* (Albuquerque, New Mexico: Inter-Hemispheric Education Resource Center, 1986), p. 27; *Labor Report on Central America*, Sept./Oct. 1985, p. 2; *Chicago Reader*, Feb. 2, 1979; Philip Agee, *Inside the Company: CIA Diary* (New York: Stonehill Publishing Co., 1975), p. 341; telephone interview with staff member at Thomas H. Miner and Associates, Chicago, Illinois.

215. *Washington Times*, May 8, 1985, p. 1; Barry, Preusch and Sims, pp. 27, 57; *World Affairs*, Winter 1983–84.

216. Diamond, p. 17; Barry, Preusch and Sims, pp. 49–50; *Guardian*, Sept. 17, 1986; *Sojourners*, Oct. 1985.

217. *Newsweek*, June 17, 1985; Barry, Preusch and Sims, p. 50; Holly Sklar, *Washington's War on Nicaragua* (Boston: South End Press, 1988), p. 241.

218. Conservative Caucus fundraising appeal, n.d.

219. U.S., Joint Hearings Before the Senate Select Committee on Secret Military Assistance to Iran and the Nicaraguan Opposition; and the House Select Committee to Investigate Covert Arms Transactions with Iran, *Iran-Contra Investigation*, Testimony of Joe Coors, 100th Cong., 1st Sess., May 20, 21, 27 and 28, 1987 (Washington, D.C.: GPO, 1988), pp. 124–129.

220. U.S., S. Rept. No. 100–216 and H. Rept. No. 100–433, *Report of the Congressional Committees Investigating the Iran-Contra Affair With Supplemental, Minority and Additional Views*, 100th Cong., 1st Sess. (Washington: GPO, 1987), p. 97.

221. 18 USC sec. 960.

222. *Labor Report on Central America*, Sept./Oct. 1985; Barry, Preusch and Sims, p. 27; *In These Times*, Aug. 3–16, 1988.

223. *The Nation*, April 15, 1978, pp. 435–36.

224. *Rocky Mountain News*, Dec. 30, 1986; *Time*, Dec. 26, 1977, p. 15.

225. *Rocky Mountain News*, July 10, 1977.

226. "Boycott Coors" statement, Michigan State AFL-CIO, Lansing, Michigan, n.d.

227. *The Nation*, April 15, 1978, pp. 434–35; Coors letter, April 6, 1977.

228. *Rocky Mountain News*, May 12, 1978.

229. Letter from W.K. Coors to Thomas Donahue, Dec. 3, 1981; letter from Donahue to Coors, Feb. 8, 1982.

230. "Boycott Coors" statement, Michigan State AFL-CIO, Lansing, Michigan, n.d.

231. Karin Chenoweth, *A Hidden Agenda: The National Right to Work Committee and Its Campaign to Undermine American Trade Unions* (New York: League for Industrial Democracy, n.d.); *RUB (Report on Union Busters) Sheet*, May 1985, p.6.

232. *Denver Monthly*, June 1979; *RUB Sheet*, May 1985, p. 6.

233. Telephone interview with staff member at USIC, Aug. 8, 1989; "The Council Difference," USIC promotional material, received 1989.

234. *Kansas City Star*, June 17, 1984, p. 4.

235. *Westword*, Sept. 4–10, 1985.

236. *Rocky Mountain News*, Aug. 24, 1984.

237. *Kansas City Star*, June 17, 1984; *Westword*, Sept. 4–10, 1985; *Rocky Mountain News*, Aug. 24, 1984.

238. *Westword*, March 22–28, 1989, p. 12.

239. *Reader's Digest*, July 19, 1983, p. 59.

240. *Rocky Mountain News*, March/April, 1981, p. 29; Jeff Stein, "The President's Men: Part II," *Penthouse*, July 1981, p. 58.

241. *Rocky Mountain Magazine*, March/April 1981, p. 29; Ron Arnold, *At the Eye of the Storm: James Watt and the Environmentalists* (Chicago, Illinois: Regnery Gateway, 1982), pp. 224, 277.

242. *Penthouse*, July 1981, pp. 58–60.

243. *Ibid*, p. 60.

244. *Chicago Tribune*, March 7, 1983, pp. 1, 5; *Reader's Digest*, July 18, 1983, p. 60.

245. *The New York Times*, Sept. 6, 1981; *Reader's Digest*, July 18, 1983, p. 60.

246. *Chicago Tribune*, March 7, 1985, p. 5.

247. *National Catholic Reporter*, March 25, 1983, p. 1.

248. *Chicago Tribune*, March 7, 1983, pp. 1, 5.

249. *National Catholic Reporter*, March 25, 1983, p. 1.

250. Arnold, p. 25.

251. Author's interviews with former LaRouche network organizers; Arnold, pp. 224, 277; Dennis King, *Lyndon LaRouche and the New American Fascism* (New York: Doubleday, 1989), p. 128.

252. Coors Foundation, IRS 990–PF, 1980, 1981; *Vancouver Sun* (British Columbia), July 8, 1989, p. A6. Thanks to Dan Junas of the Institute for Global Security Studies in Seattle for bringing this article to my attention.

253. Charles L. Heatherly, ed., *Mandate for Leadership* (Washington, D.C.: Heritage Foundation, 1981), pp. 333, 345–46, 372–73; Arnold, pp. 21, 271.

254. Richard N. Holwill, ed., *Agenda '83* (Washington, D.C.: Heritage Foundation, 1983), pp. 181–191, 333, 339. The author of the report is also listed as Gale Norton.

255. This section on Coors' TVN is based primarily on an excellent study of the organization: Stanhope Gould, "Coors Brews the News," *Columbia Journalism Review*, March/April 1975, pp. 17–29.

256. *Ibid.*

257. Adolph Coors Foundation Annual Report, 1988; *Mother Jones*, July 1984, p. 5.

258. U.S., House, Committee on International Relations, Subcommittee on International Organizations, *Investigation of Korean-American Relations*, 95th Cong., 2nd Sess., Oct. 31, 1978, p. 369.

259. *Chronicle of Higher Education*, Dec. 12, 1985, p. 19; *The Forerunner*, Sept. 1985; *Village Voice*, Aug. 13, 1985, p. 8.

260. Adolph Coors Foundation Annual Report, 1988; Coors Foundation, IRS 990–PF, 1988.

261. *The New York Times Magazine*, Feb. 26, 1989; *New York Times*, March 29, 1988; IEA Annual Report, 1988.

262. IEA Annual Report, 1988, p. 9. IEA has been known as the Madison Center since Sept. 1990 when the two groups merged.

263. *Ibid.*, p. 10.

264. *Washington Post*, Sept. 24, 1985, p. 10.

265. IEA Annual Report, 1988, p. 5.

266. *Ibid.*

267. This section on the Gablers is based on a variety of sources. See, for example, Barbara Parker, "Your Schools May Be the Next Battlefield in the Crusade Against 'Improper' Textbooks," *American School Board Journal*, June 1979; *San Jose Mercury*, Aug. 25, 1982; *Washington Post*, April 3, 1982; *The Texas Project of People for the American Way* (Austin, Texas: People for the American Way, September 21, 1982); and *As Texas Goes, So Goes the Nation: A Report on Textbook Selection in Texas* (Austin, Texas: People for the American Way, 1983). For an admiring look at the Gablers, see James C. Hefley, *Textbooks on Trial: The Informative Report of Mel and Norma Gabler's ongoing Battle to Oust Objectionable Textbooks from Public Schools* (Wheaton, IL: SP Publications, 1976, 1977).

268. Thanks to Margaret Quigley of Political Research Associates for research work on this section, particularly on Hillsdale College, including her attendance at events sponsored by the College to collect the documents discussed here.

269. John Ranelagh, *The Agency: The Rise and Decline of the CIA* (New York: Simon and Schuster, 1986), p. 246n. According to Ranelagh, former CIA bureaucrat Tom Braden charged after his resignation from the CIA that *Encounter* was not

only funded by the CIA but that one of its three editors was a CIA agent. Lasky was left as sole editor at *Encounter* after his two co-editors resigned, charging that Lasky had lied to them about the source of the magazine's funds.

270. U.S. Council for World Freedom list of board and advisory board members. Author attended 1985 WACL conference.

271. George Roche, "The Price of Independence," *Imprimis*, Jan. 1989, p. 4.

272. George Roche, *Education in America* (Hillsdale, MI: Hillsdale College Press, 1977), p. 153.

273. George Roche, *One By One: Preserving Values and Freedom in Heartland America* (Hillsdale, MI: Hillsdale College Press, 1990), p. 203.

274. Gerda Bikales, "Maximum Feasible Misunderstanding: Bilingual Education in Our Schools," *Imprimis*, Oct. 1989, p. 1.

275. *Imprimis*, June 1984. On Ayau, see Jenny Pearce, *Under the Eagle* (Boston: South End Press, 1982), pp. 178, 180. On Belli, see also author's articles in *National Catholic Reporter*, Nov. 18, 1988, p. 1.

276. Samuel L. Blumenfeld, "Who Killed Excellence?" *Imprimis*, Sept. 1985.

277. Samuel L. Blumenfeld, *Is Public Education Necessary?* (Old Greenwich, CT: Devin-Adair, 1981), p. x.

278. *Ibid.*

279. *Issues '88* (Washington, D.C.: Free Congress Education and Research Foundation, 1988), pp. 89–90.

280. Accuracy in Academia Conference Flyer, undated, received May 15, 1991.

281. *Ibid.*

282. Allan Brownfield, "Western Culture: Common Patrimony Among Us All," *Campus Report*, April 1991, p. 7.

283. *Campus Report*, Jan. 1991, p. 5; *Campus Report*, Dec. 1990, p. 7.

284. *Campus Report*, Feb. 1991, p. 1.

285. IRS Form 990, Adolph A. Coors foundation; foundation reports.

286. *The New York Times*, May 16, 1989, p. 1.

287. *Ibid.*

APPENDIX 1

Selected Grants:
Adolph Coors Foundation
Annual Report, 1988

HEALTH GRANTS

American Council on Science and Health, $25,000
Help underwrite distribution of "Big Fears . . . Little Risks," a documentary on
man-made chemicals.

Colorado Business Coalition for Health, $50,000
Expansion of program which promotes positive changes in the providing and
purchasing of health care.

EDUCATION GRANTS

CBN University, $50,000
General Support.

Christendom College, $5,000
General Support.

Colorado Council on Economic Education, $30,000
Program fosters a greater understanding and awareness of economics among
teachers and clergy throughout Colorado.

Colorado School of Mines Foundation, $252,414
Final portion of three-year grant challenging alumni giving. Herman F. Coors
Professorial Chair in Ceramics.

Denver Entrepreneurship Academy, $4,500
Promotes entrepreneurial skills among college students interested in pursuing a
variety of professions.

Educational Research Analysts, $20,000
Review of educational materials.

Hillsdale College, $40,000
Center for Constructive Alternatives.

National Association of Christian Educators, $15,000
Program stresses moral and academic excellence in schools.

Students in Free Enterprise, $5,000
Campus program increases students' awareness and understanding of the principles
of the free enterprise system.

YOUTH

Colorado Alliance of Business, $25,000
Work for Yourself Program expansion in Grand Junction and Pueblo; program
helps students develop entrepreneurial skills for job alternatives.

Leaders of Tomorrow, $2,000
1988 high school journalism program designed to give students insight into the
workings of the free enterprise system and the role and responsibilities of the press.

Leadership Institute, $20,000
Nationwide recruitment efforts and support of program that identifies and trains
young leaders.

Students for America, $15,000
Campus student group promoting conservative viewpoints.

CIVIC AND CULTURAL

Ronald Reagan Presidential Foundation, $50,000
Building of Reagan Presidential Library.

PUBLIC AFFAIRS

Accuracy in Academia, $10,000
Support of programs promoting balanced teaching practices on university
campuses.

Accuracy in Media, $20,000
Promotes accuracy and fairness in news reporting.

American Defense Institute, $5,000
Programs raise awareness of national defense needs.

American Foundation for Resistance International, $10,000
Support of program activities in the U.S.

American Spectator Educational Foundation, $10,000
Publication of *American Spectator*.

Capital Research Center, $20,000
Education and research activities focus on the role of policy organizations.

Center for Media and Public Affairs, $20,000
Evaluates the impact of media on public opinion.

Center for Peace and Freedom, $25,000
Educates the public and U.S. policymakers about national security issues.

Colorado Association of Commerce and Industry, $25,000
Educational Foundation Blueprint for Colorado's Future, a long-term agenda for Colorado's growth.

Council for National Policy, $5,000
Convenes meetings of national leaders to discuss public policy issues.

Education and Research Institute, $25,000
Support of the National Journalism Center which trains future journalists.

Ethics and Public Policy Center, $30,000
Research activities focus on religious and ethical aspects of public policy.

Free Congress Research and Education Foundation, $150,000
Program activities help shape conservative policy reform.

Freedoms Foundation at Valley Forge, $25,000
Communication program for free enterprise education.

Heritage Foundation, $100,000
Conducts research and educational activities on major public policy issues.

Hoover Institution, $30,000
Analysis and research of public policy issues.

Hudson Institution, $25,000
Programs involve U.S. foreign policy issues, economic growth and defense.

Independence Institute, $25,000
Public policy center addressing pertinent issues facing Colorado.

Institute for Educational Affairs, $10,000
Publishes and distributes information on American culture and political traditions.

Institute for Research on the Economics of Taxation, $5,000
Programs provide free market perspective on economic policy issues.

Intercollegiate Studies Institute, $10,000
Provides college students and professors with information on free enterprise.

Jamestown Foundation, $10,000
General support.

Landmark Legal Foundation, $20,000
Public interest law firm.

Manhattan Institute for Policy Research, $5,000
Enhances understanding of economic issues and policies by distributing research findings.

Mid-America Legal Foundation, $5,000
Public interest law firm.

Morality in Media, $15,000
Promotes enforcement of federal obscenity laws.

National Center for Policy Analysis, $5,000
Pro-free enterprise public policy research institute exploring innovative solutions to current problems.

National Center for Public Policy Research, $25,000
Assists the development of grass roots organizations which promote the principles of a free society.

National Forum Foundation, $50,000
Program activities targeted to policy issues relating to family, welfare reform, and national security.

National Institute for Public Policy, $10,000
Provides information on national security issues.

National Legal Center for the Public Interest, $20,000
Focuses on issues and policies pertaining to the judicial branch of government.

National Strategy Information Center, $20,000
Programs and publications provide information on international security.

Pacific Legal Foundation, $20,000
Public interest law firm.

Pacific Research Institute for Public Policy, $5,000
Evaluates the consequences of government policies and provides constructive policy reform ideas.

Philadelphia Society, $2,500
Efforts broaden the understanding of the principles and traditions of a free society.

Rockford Institute, $40,000
Program activities promote a free society.

SSC Partnership Corporation, $36,000
Efforts increase public's understanding of Super Conductor technology and promote Colorado as a site in which to locate a facility.

Social Philosophy and Policy Center, $5,000
Explores the moral and economic case for the free market system.

Southeastern Legal Foundation, $5,000
Public interest law firm.

Students for a Better America, $2,500
Student group representing a conservative philosophy on college campuses.

U. S. Industrial Council Educational Foundation, $5,000
Support of Colorado activities.

Washington Legal Foundation, $30,000
Public interest law firm.

RELIGIOUS GRANTS

A Christian Ministry in the National Parks, $10,000
Provides worship services, religious activities, and Christian education for visitors and employees in the national parks.

Institute on Religion and Democracy, $15,000
Conducts research on religious issues and activities.

Intercessors for America, $5,000
Activities promote restoration of good government and biblical family life.

Rutherford Institute, $10,000
Defends religious liberties and provides a forum for public awareness of issues facing the religious community.

APPENDIX 2

Free Congress Foundation
Top Fifteen Lifetime Donors as of 1988

Scaife Foundation (R.M. Scaife), $3,507,000

Carthage Foundation (R.M. Scaife), $3,507,000

J.M. Foundation, $995,000

Bradley Foundation, $900,760

Krieble Family – Robert and Nancy [Loctite Corp.], $537,996

Milliken, Mr. and Mrs. Roger – Romill Foundation, $500,000

Coors – Joseph, Sr. and Coors Foundation, $485,000

Olin Foundation, $448,000

Follansbee, Nancy Avery, $239,441

DeMoss, Nancy, $235,000

Valerio, Michael and Helen (Papa Gino's), $230,177

Noble Foundation, $180,000

Lennon, Fred A. – (Foundation), $156,000

Ahmanson, Howard Jr. (Fieldstead Foundation), $152,000

DeVos Foundation – Richard and Helen [Amway Corp.], $105,500

Note: names in square brackets are for identification and reference purposes only and may not relate to donations in any way.

APPENDIX 3

Organizations and Acronyms

AIA Accuracy in Academia

AIM Accuracy in Media

ACLU American Civil Liberties Union

AFC American Freedom Coalition

AIP American Independent Party

ASC American Security Council

ASCF American Security Council Foundation

ABN Anti-Bolshevik Bloc of Nations

BLM Bureau of Land Management

CBN Christian Broadcast Network

CDU Christian Democratic Union

CIA Central Intelligence Agency

CFA Coalitions for America

CFR Council on Foreign Relations

CV Christian Voice

CUT Church Universal and Triumphant

CIS Council for Inter-American Security

CMA Civilian Military Assistance

CN Collegiate Network

CNP Council for National Policy

CPTS Coalition for Peace Through Strength

CRF Coalition for Religious Freedom

COR Coalition on Revival

CSFC Committee for the Survival of a Free Congress

CWA Concerned Women for America

CUFE Council for a Union-Free Environment

CAA Council on American Affairs

DANK German American National Congress

MDF Democratic Forum

DOD Department of Defense

HUD Department of Housing and Urban Development

EEOC Equal Employment Opportunity Commission (EEOC)

EPA Environmental Protection Agency

ERA Equal Rights Amendment

FAIR Federation for American Immigration Reform

FLF Freedom Leadership Foundation

FCF Free Congress Foundation

IHR Institute for Historical Review

ICE Institute for Christian Economics

IFA Intercessors for America

INSI Institute for North South Issues

IRD Institute on Religion and Democracy

ISEI Inter-American Security Educational Foundation

IRS Internal Revenue Service

IPF International Policy Forum

JBS John Birch Society

KCIA Korean Central Intelligence Agency

KKK Ku Klux Klan

MSLF Mountain States Legal Foundation

NACE National Association of Christian Educators

NAP New Alliance Party

NRTWC National Right to Work Committee

NED National Endowment for Democracy

NSC National Security Council

NSIC National Strategy Information Center

NCAC National Christian Action Coalition

NCPAC National Conservative Political Action Committee

NFF Nicaraguan Freedom Foundation

NSI North South Institute

OSHA Occupational Safety and Health Administration

OUN Organization of Ukrainian Nationalists

PAY Patriotic American Youth

TFP Society for the Defense of Tradition, Family, and Property

USIC United States Industrial Council

USCWF United States Council for World Freedom

USIA United States Information Agency

UCCA Ukrainian Congress Committee of America

WACL World Anti-Communist League

WOG Word of God

INDEX

A

A Christian Ministry in the National
  Parks—85, 129.
ABN
  See Anti-Bolshevik Bloc of Nations
  (ABN)
ABN Correspondence—35.
Abortion—17–18, 40, 56, 59, 60–61.
Academic License—100.
Accuracy in Academia (AIA)—93, 99–100,
  126.
Accuracy in Media (AIM)—91, 93, 100,
  126.
ACLU
  See American Civil Liberties
  Union (ACLU)
*ACLU: One of the Most Harmful
  Organizations in America, The*
  (LaHaye)–56.
Acquired Immune Deficiency Syndrome
  (AIDS)—xv, 22, 62–63.
  and mandatory testing—61.
  and quarantine—63.
  See also Children with AIDS
    Foundation
  See also HIV antibodies and mandatory
    testing
Adolph Coors Company—xiii.
  subsidiaries—xiii.
Adultery—57, 60.
  to be punished by execution—40.

AFC
  See American Freedom Coalition (AFC)
Affirmative action—70, 95, 98, 100.
Afghanistan—13, 28, 76.
  and Fundamentalism—25, 76.
AFL-CIO—17, 80–82, 84.
Africa—13, 20, 32, 67, 76.
African-Americans (Black Americans)—
  xiv, 3, 17, 66, 68, 70, 72, 74, 92, 94, 96,
  100.
  genetic inferiority alleged—5, 38, 100.
  See also Civil rights
  See also Racist
  See also Segregation
  targeted by Coors advertising—vii,
    73–74.
Agnew, Spiro—90.
Ahmanson, Howard Jr.—130.
AIA
  See Accuracy in Academia (AIA)
AIDS
  See Acquired Immune Deficiency
  Syndrome (AIDS)
Ailes, Roger—91.
AIM
  See Accuracy in Media (AIM)
AIP
  See American Independent Party (AIP)
Aker, Frank—37.
Allies for Renewal—19.
Allot, Gordon—2, 15.
Alvor accords—39.
Amalgamated Clothing & Textile Workers
  Union—viii.

American Civil Liberties Union (ACLU)—
56.
American Coalition for Life—20.
American Conservative Union—iii.
American Council on Science and
Health—125.
American Defense Institute—127.
American Foreign Policy Institute—49.
American Foundation for Resistance
International—127.
American Freedom Coalition (AFC)—9,
21, 40, 89.
American Independent Party (AIP)—
16–17, 40, 53.
American Opinion—42, 45.
American Security Council (ASC)—22, 25,
32, 48–50, 82.
Coalition for Peace through Strength—
48–49.
American Security Council Foundation
(ASCF)—48–49, 51.
American Society of Local Officials—75.
American Spectator, The—93, 127.
American Spectator Educational
Foundation—127.
Americans for Robertson—50.
Amherst Spectator—92.
Amigos del Pais—99.
Amoco Oil—86.
Amway Corporation—27, 38, 54, 130.
called morally and criminally corrupt—
27.
Analysis and Research, Inc.—1.
Anatole Alert—20.
Anatole Fellowship—19–20.
Andrews, John—74.
Angeline, Debra—viii.
Angola—xv, 13, 20, 28, 39, 53, 77, 103.
Ann Arbor, Michigan—18, 92.
Anti-Bolshevik Bloc of Nations (ABN)—
12, 34–35.
Antichrist—30, 117.
Anti-communism—32, 43.
Anti-Jewish
See Anti-Semitism
Anti-Semitism—2, 7, 31–32, 35.
activity in Coors funded groups—v, xiv,
103.
American Independent Party (AIP)—
17.
Coalition for Peace Through Strength—
49.
Liberty Lobby—4, 71.
Rockford Institute—101.
Ukrainian Congress Committee of
America—31.

Wildmon, Don—43.
World Anti-Communist League
(WACL)—28.
Antitrust—11, 13.
Apartheid—38, 52–53, 67, 74.
Apocalypse—18.
Argentina—25, 76.
Arizona—27.
Armageddon—62.
Armstrong, William—27, 29, 33.
Arnold, Ron—88–89.
Arrow Cross—31–32.
ASC
See American Security Council (ASC)
ASCF
See American Security Council
Foundation (ASCF)
Asia—6, 13, 32, 75.
Asian Studies Center—6.
Aspin, Les—17.
Assassination—47, 48.
Astrologers to be punished by execution—
40.
*At the Eye of the Storm: James Watt and the
Environmentalists* (Arnold)—88.
Atlantic Monthly—10, 13, 16.
Attack on the Americas—49.
Australia—27.
Authoritarianism—v, 23, 48, 103.
Avon Products—27.
Ayau, Manuel—99.
Aztec culture—74.

B

Badger Herald—92.
Baltic Region—34.
Barbie, Klaus—76.
Barker, Clifford—45.
Barnett, Frank—47.
Barnum, P.T.—96.
Baton Rouge, Louisiana—37.
Bavaria—90.
Beatles, The—39.
Beckett, Ian—30.
Beckett, John D.—26, 30, 33, 54.
Bellant, Russ—vii, viii.
Bellevue, Washington—89.
Belli, Humberto—99.
Bendetsen, Karl—49.
Bennett, William—21, 94.
Berlet, Chip—v, vii–viii.
Berlin—31.
Bestiality—57, 60.

Better Business Bureau—54.
Bible—40, 57, 95–96.
    literal interpretation of biblical law—21.
Bikales, Gerda—98–99.
Bilingual education—99.
    alleged tie to terrorism—74.
Billings, Robert—17–18, 26, 29, 33, 70.
Binghamton Times—92.
Birth control
    See Contraception
Black Americans
    See African-Americans (Black
        Americans)
Black, Edwin—49.
Blackburn, Ben—3, 39, 71.
Blacklisting—95.
    and American Security Council—49.
    of liberal speakers by USIA—94.
Blackwell, Morton—20–21, 36, 40, 43.
Blasphemers—57, 66.
    to be punished by execution—40.
BLM
    See Bureau of Land Management (BLM)
Blumenfeld, Samuel—99.
Bo Hi Pak—117.
Bob Jones University—70.
Boilermakers Union—81.
Bolivia—76.
Borchelt, Harry—82.
Bork, Robert—94.
Boston, Massachusetts—63.
    opposition to busing—71.
Boston City Hospital—63.
Boston College—92.
Boston College Observer—92.
Botha, Pik—26.
Bouchey, L. Francis (Lynn)—37.
Boycotts of Coors products—66–67, 72,
    80–81, 84, 103.
Braden, Tom—122.
Bradley Foundation—130.
Brady, Tom—72.
Braham, Randolph L.—32, 111–112.
Brandeis University—92.
Brandeisian—92.
Brandt, Willy—2.
Brewers Union—80.
Brewery Workers Local 366—80, 84.
Brillo pad
    term used in racist manner—92, 94.
Britain
    See England
Brown, Robert K.—43.
Brown Spectator—92.
Brown University—92.
Brown v. Board of Education—72.

Buchanan, Pat—9.
Buckley, William F.—97.
Bulgaria—34.
Bureau of Land Management (BLM)—87.
Burford, Anne Gorsuch—87, 90.
Burford, Robert—87, 90.
Bush Administration—vi, 32–33, 54, 86,
    93.
Bush, President George—62, 90.
    anti-Semites and fascists in 1988
        campaign—31.
Busing—iii, 45, 71, 96.
    and John Birch Society—45.
Butler, Stuart M.—4–5.
Byelorussia—34.

C

CAA
    See Council on American Affairs
        (CAA)
Cabinet
    "shadow cabinet"—53.
    Kitchen Cabinet—9–10, 55.
    Reagan Administration—88.
Calero, Adolpho—75.
California—1, 13, 66, 75, 85.
    Costa Mesa—20.
    Orange County—19.
    Malibu—101.
    Santa Clara County (Silicon Valley)—
        19.
    Santa Rosa—19.
California Chamber of Commerce—85.
California Review—92.
Cambodia—25, 28.
Cambridge, Massachusetts—vii.
Campus Report—100.
Campus Review—92.
Canada—30, 71, 89.
Capital Research Center—127.
Capitol Hill—2, 4, 13, 35, 54.
Carbone, Leslie—100.
Carleton College—92.
Carleton Observer—92.
Carlson, Allan—101.
Carolina Critic—92.
Carroll, Warren—26.
Carter Administration—53, 87, 89.
Carthage Foundation—vi, 130.
Carto, Willis—4.
Casey, William—76, 79, 115.
Catholic (Roman Catholic Church)—2, 18,
    21–23, 26.

Catholic Conference—22.

CBN

   See Christian Broadcast Network (CBN)

CBN University

   See Regent University (formerly CBN University)

CDU

   See Christian Democratic Union (CDU)

Censorship—11.

   textbook—3, 7, 71, 95–97.

Center for Catholic Policy—22.

Center for Child and Family Policy—21.

Center for Conservative Governance—21.

Center for Constructive Alternatives (CCA)

   See Hillsdale College

Center for Cultural Conservatism—21.

Center for the Defense of Free Enterprise—89.

Center for Foreign Policy—22.

Center for Government and Politics—21.

Center for International Security Studies—49.

Center for Judicial Studies—71.

Center for Law and Democracy—21.

Center for Media and Public Affairs—127.

Center for Pastoral Renewal—22.

Center for Peace and Freedom—127.

Center for State Policy—21.

Center for Transportation Policy—22.

Central America—13, 20, 22, 32, 49–50, 76, 99.

Central Intelligence Agency (CIA)—11, 23, 25–26, 48–49, 76, 79, 97, 99.

CFA

   See Coalitions for America (CFA)

CFR

   See Council on Foreign Relations (CFR)

Chamber of Commerce—25, 85.

Chancey, Susie—viii.

Chang Se Tong—6.

Channell, Spitz—79.

Charleston, West Virginia—3.

Charleston Gazette—viii.

Chastity—56.

Chemical Waste Management—88.

Chevron Oil—86.

Chicago, Illinois—72, 88.

Chicago Crucible—92.

Chicanos—xiv, 72–74.

   anti-Chicano—75.

Children

   and abuse—56, 61.

   and molestation—56.

   and nutrition—12.

   mandatory testing for HIV antibodies—61, 63.

   to be punished by execution—40.

Children with AIDS Foundation—38.

Chile—22, 25.

Choice Not an Echo, A (Schlafly)—43.

Christendom College—26, 100, 125.

Christian—18–21, 26, 30, 35, 40, 43, 57, 70, 95–96.

   Christian republic—18, 21, 27.

   fundamentalism—28, 30, 39, 62.

   "muscular" Christianity advocated—19.

   slavery—40.

   warriors—20.

Christian Broadcast Network (CBN)—50, 76.

Christian Crusade—39.

Christian Democratic Union (CDU)—90.

Christian Front—2.

Christian Reconstruction Movement—20–21, 39–40, 50.

   Coors support for—xv.

Christian Science Monitor—67.

Christian Social Union—90.

Christian Voice (CV)—9, 19, 40.

Christianity Today—40.

Chun Doo Hwan—6.

Church Universal and Triumphant (CUT)—38.

CIA

   See Central Intelligence Agency (CIA)

Cies, William—45.

CIS

   See Council for Inter-American Security (CIS)

Citizen's Councils—72.

Citizens Cabinet Organizing Committee—53.

Citizens for America—77.

Civil rights—viii, 3, 39, 42, 44–45, 70–72, 74, 103.

Civil Rights Act—67, 98.

Civil Rights Commission—66.

Civil service employees—11.

Civilian Military Assistance (CMA)—79.

Claremont Independent—92.

Cline, Ray—49.

CMA

   See Civilian Military Assistance (CMA)

CN

   See Collegiate Network (CN)

CNP

   See Council for National Policy (CNP)

CNP, Inc.—36.

Coalition Against English Only—viii.

Coalition for Freedom—54.

Regent University—76.
Washington Legal Foundation—11.
Coors Political Action Committee—103.
Coors Porcelain Company—xiii, 84.
Coors Technology Companies—xiii.
Coors, Adolph, IV—xiii.
Coors, Adolph, Jr.—xiii.
Coors, Adolph, Sr.—xiii.
Coors, Grover—xiii.
Coors, Herman F.—126.
Coors, Holly—v–vi, xv, 17–18, 37–38, 46, 50, 53–55, 62, 74, 76–77, 85, 100.
Coors, Jeffrey—v–vi, xiii–xv, 17–18, 33, 35, 46, 62–63, 66, 86, 97, 103–104.
Coors, Joe—iii, vi–vii, xiii–xv, 1–2, 9–10, 13, 16–18, 35, 37, 45–50, 53–56, 60, 62–63, 66, 72–74, 76–81, 84–90, 101, 130.
Coors, Joseph, Jr.—xiii–xiv, 62.
Coors, Peter—vi, xiii–xv, 17–18, 35, 55, 81, 103.
Coors, William—vi, xiii, xv, 35, 55–56, 67, 74, 81–82.
and racism—67.
COR
See Coalition on Revival (COR)
Cornell Review—92.
Cornell University—55.
Coronet Foods—27.
Costa Mesa, California—20.
Coughlin, Father Charles—2–3, 7.
Council for a Union-Free Environment (CUFE)—82.
Council for Inter-American Security (CIS)—74–75.
and Rev. Moon—37.
Council for National Policy (CNP)—v, xiv, 3, 13, 20–21, 26–27, 29, 36–43, 45–46, 54, 56, 63, 74–75, 82, 98, 101, 127.
Council on American Affairs (CAA)—4–5, 49.
Council on Foreign Relations (CFR)—37, 43–45.
Couple to Couple League International—60.
Covert Action Information Bulletin—viii.
Covert operations—12, 48–49.
covert action—48.
funding—25, 76.
warfare—44.
Cowan, Mark—84.
CPTS
See Coalition for Peace Through Strength (CPTS)
Crane, Philip—2–3, 97.

Crawford, Alan—iii, 1–3, 15, 45.
Creationism—95.
CRF
See Coalition for Religious Freedom (CRF)
CSFC
See Committee for the Survival of a Free Congress (CSFC)
Csorba, Les—93.
Csurka, Istvan—35.
CUFE
See Council for a Union-Free Environment (CUFE)
Cultural Conservatism—19.
Curtis, Senator Carl—91.
CUT
See Church Universal and Triumphant (CUT)
CV
See Christian Voice (CV)
CWA
See Concerned Women for America (CWA)
Czechoslovakia—32.

D

D'Onofrio, William—39.
Dallas, Texas—98.
DANK
See German American National Congress (DANK)
Dartmouth College—92, 94.
Dartmouth Review—92, 94.
Davis, T. Cullen—37.
Dawidowicz, Lucy—39.
Day-care, conservative opposition to—56.
De Borchgrave, Arnaud—9.
Death penalty
See Executions
Death squads—4, 75–76, 78, 99.
DeBey, Ken—viii.
Decertification election—81.
DeGaulle, Charles—28.
Democracy—xv, 22, 44, 95, 103–104.
anti-democratic forces—4, 21, 23.
called heresy—40.
end sought by Moon—9.
to be replaced by theocracy—21, 39–40.
Democratic Forum (MDF)—35.
Democratic Party—18, 83.
Democratic pluralism—v, 95, 103–104.
Demonist—40.

G

H

I

IEA
    See Institute for Educational Affairs
    (IEA)
IFA
    See Intercessors for America (IFA)
IHR
    See Institute for Historical Review
    (IHR)
Idaho—85.
Ideas Have Consequences (Hillsdale)—97.
Ideology—3, 50, 81, 91, 95.
    National socialist—31, 34.
Illiberal Education—99.
Illini Review—92.
Illinois—38.
    Chicago—72, 88.
Immigrants—75.
Imprimis—97–99.
Independence Institute—74–75, 127.
Indiana—54, 97.
    Ku Klux Klan—38.
Indianapolis, Indiana—54.
Industrial waste dumps—87.
Inquisition
    See Spanish Inquisition
INSI
    See Institute for North South Issues
    (INSI)
Inside the League (Anderson and
    Anderson)—4, 78.
Institute for Christian Economics (ICE)—
    40.
    See also Christian Reconstruction
        Movement
Institute for Educational Affairs (IEA)—
    92–94, 101, 122, 127.
Institute for Global Security Studies—121.
Institute for Historical Review (IHR)—4.
    See also Historical Revisionism
Institute for North South Issues (INSI)—
    79.
Institute for Research on the Economics of
    Taxation—127.
Institute on Religion and Democracy
    (IRD)—50, 129.
Integration—39, 96.
Intelligence agencies—46, 48, 75–76.
    Korean—5–6, 9, 93.
    South African military—67.
Intelligence gathering
    by Western Goals—45.
Inter-American Security Educational
    Institute (ISEI)—74–75.
Intercessors for America (IFA)—26–27, 30,
    129.
Intercollegiate Studies Institute—100, 128.

Internal Revenue Service (IRS)—2, 70.
International Cultural Foundation—6.
International Oceanic Enterprises—6.
International Policy Forum (IPF)—22, 25,
    27, 40.
International Workers Party (IWP)—107.
Interracial
    dating—70.
    marriage—38.
IPF
    See International Policy Forum (IPF)
Iran-Contra—37, 48, 79.
    See also Contras
IRD
    See Institute on Religion and
    Democracy (IRD)
Ironworkers Union—81.
IRS
    See Internal Revenue Service (IRS)
Irvine, Reed—21, 91, 93, 100.
ISEI
    See Inter-American Security
    Educational Institute (ISEI)
Islamic Fundamentalists—25, 28, 76.
Issues '88: A Platform for America (Free
    Congress and Heritage Foundations)—
    60–62, 86.
Italian fascist movements—4.
Ivon, David—viii.
IWP
    See International Workers Party (IWP)

J

J.M. Foundation—130.
Jackson, Mississippi—72.
Jamba, Angola—53.
Jamestown Foundation—128.
Japanese team concepts—84.
Japanese-Americans
    internment of—49.
Jarmin, Gary—9.
JBS
    See John Birch Society (JBS)
Jefferson, Thomas—96.
Jenkins, Louis (Woody)—37, 54.
Jensen, Arthur—38.
Jews—57.
    attacks on in U.S.—2.
    Holocaust—4, 32, 43.
    See also Anti-Semitism

K

L

White House—10, 21, 32, 37, 50, 76–77, 93.
White House Office of Public Liaison—27.
White House Outreach Working Group on Central America—28.
White supremacy
    See Racist
Whittlesey, Faith Ryan—27–28, 33.
Wilderness—87, 89.
Wilderness Act—89.
Wildlife refuges—88.
Wildmon, Rev. Don—43.
Will They Listen Now? (Manion)—98.
William and Mary College—92.
Williams Observer—92.
Wilson, Jack—1, 16, 90–91, 93.
Wisconsin—2, 17.
WOG
    See Word of God (WOG)
Wolf, Lou—viii.
Wombats
    term used in sexist manner—92, 94.
Women—v, 92, 94, 100, 103.
    and the John Birch Society—45.
    women's liberation—iii, xiv, 96.
    feminization of poverty—60.
Word of God (WOG)—18–19, 22, 60.
World Affairs—76.
World Anti-Communist League (WACL)—4–5, 13, 25, 28, 34–35, 37, 49, 71, 75–78, 98.
    Links to Moon's Unification Church network—6.
World War II—2, 12, 25, 28, 31, 34–35, 49.
Wyoming—88.

X

X, Rick—viii.
Xenophobia—v, 101.

Y

Yale Free Press—92.
Yale Political Magazine—92.
Yale University—92.

Z

Zimbabwe—67.
Zionism—17.

ABOUT SOUTH END PRESS

South End Press is a nonprofit, collectively run book publisher with over 150 titles in print. Since our founding in 1977, we have tried to meet the needs of readers who are exploring, or are already committed to, the politics of radical social change.

Our goal is to publish books that encourage critical thinking and constructive action on the key political, cultural, social, economic, and ecological issues shaping life in the United States and in the world. In this way, we hope to give expression to a wide diversity of democratic social movements and to provide an alternative to the products of corporate publishing.

If you would like a free catalog of South End Press books or information about our membership program—which offers two free books and a 40% discount on all titles—please write us at South End Press, 116 Saint Botolph Street, Boston, MA 02115.

OTHER TITLES OF INTEREST FROM SOUTH END PRESS

Old Nazis, The New Right, and the Republican Party:
Domestic Fascist Networks and U.S. Cold War Politics
Russ Bellant

COINTELPRO Papers:
Documents from the FBI's Secret Wars Against Dissent in the United States
Ward Churchill and Jim Vander Wall

Race, Gender, and Work:
A Multi-cultural Economic History of Women in the United States
Teresa Amott and Julie Matthaei

The Praetorian Guard:
The U.S. Role in the New World Order
John Stockwell

Yearning:
Race, Gender, and Cultural Politics
bell hooks

Finding Our Way:
Rethinking Eco-feminist Politics
Janet Biehl